Lost In Yaba

Down and Out in Laos

By Walt Gleeson

Also by this author

Pattaya Youtuber: And other true stories from Thailand

1

'candy' = yaba

'gun' = drug paraphernalia

'boat' = drug paraphernalia

100,000 Kip = 10 dollars (used interchangeably)

'falang' = a foreigner in Laos

'falang town' = the foreigner area / the tourist area in Vientiane.

All the candy was gone, yet Fon stayed on the floor making boats out of the tin foil from a chewing gum packet. I lay on the bed at the opposite side of the room. CNN was playing on the TV. We had needed the sound of the TV to cover the sound of the bubbling water in the gun. More news about the BP oil spill. In Laos, the only TV channels in English were CNN and BBC, and all they ever reported was the oil spill. Now that we didn't have any candy left, I could turn off the TV and turn on the air conditioner. In recent months I had developed the habit of lying down on my stomach and resting my head on my right arm so that the left side of my chest would not push against the mattress. I wanted to keep all the pressure off the left side of my chest when I was on candy.

When I smoked my first few pills, my heart started pounding very quickly, making it impossible to sleep. After two or three days without sleep, my heartbeat became very irregular. I could feel a beat, beat, beat, then a pause (I panic) and then a beat again. The heartbeat remained fast, but it became very faint after a few days. This was my fourth day without sleep. While Fon was making boats, I lay down and tried to slow my heartbeat down a bit. I was worried. My heartbeat was so fast and faint that I couldn't even clearly distinguish the beats. All the beats flowed into one constant movement like the flow of a river. I desperately needed a few minutes to relax and let my body slow down.

"Can you turn off the air conditioner?" Fon asked.

"Why? It's hot."

"I am making boats. The air conditioner is blowing the foil away."

"Why are you making more boats? Do you have some candy left?"

Sometimes Fon kept a few candies hidden away, and then she would reveal them when we needed them most. I loved those surprises. But other times I'm sure she hid some and kept them for herself. She would often spend nearly an hour at a time in the bathroom, with the water running. I was sure she sometimes smoked a few candies on her own secretly.

"No, I don't have candy, but I will buy. I message Ting already. He is coming."

I just wanted to rest.

"Fon, I haven't slept in nearly four days. I need to sleep."

"I know. You don't do. I will do. You rest. Don't worry."

"I'm not buying anymore, really. Tell Ting not to come. Tell him we are sleeping."

5

"He outside now already. Don't worry. I buy. "

"You have money?"

"No, but Ting give me loan five candies. I pay him next time."

I was staying in an apartment in Vientiane, right next to Wat Si Muang temple. It was about a kilometer outside of falang town. There were eight apartments in the complex – four apartments on either side of a long, dark hallway. There was a high wrought iron gate in the front. The gate protected the motorbikes that were parked inside the complex, in the small courtyard at the front. Only half of the apartments were occupied. The monthly rent of one hundred and fifty dollars was far too expensive for most Lao people to afford. The apartments were probably originally built for falang tenants, but apart from me there was only one other falang in the complex – a middle-aged French guy who was living with his Lao girlfriend. The other two apartments were occupied by two young Lao women. Their falang boyfriends probably paid their rent. When I came to Laos first, I stayed in a cheap guesthouse for about six months. This apartment was nearly the same price and far more comfortable. There was a large open area with a bed, a sofa, a coffee table, a TV and a large wooden wardrobe. There were two doors at the back – one led to a large kitchen, the other door was for the bathroom. My apartment was sandwiched between two other apartments, so the only window was the one next to the front door that looked into the hallway.

When I say 'candy', I mean 'yaba'. Nobody ever said the real word for the pills, so we all used the words 'candy' or 'chocolate'. The pills look like candy and they smell like chocolate. I heard that they add the chocolate smell to the pills to make them more appealing to kids. They are small pink pills. All I know about them is that they are made in Burma and smuggled into other Southeast Asian countries. It is a popular drug because it is much cheaper than the drug 'ice', but the affects are very similar. Whereas ice is very pure and clean, candy is a dirty drug. The only two definite ingredients are amphetamines and caffeine, but anything else that is put in to make up the mixture is at the discretion of the producers in the jungles of Burma. The main thing is that it is cheap. It costs about two dollars a pill. If you just want to party, you can take one or two pills and that will be enough to make you feel good for the night. But if you get the habit bad, you might need one or two pills every couple of hours. It's not so cheap then.

The 'gun' is a plastic bottle with a small hole burnt into the side. It is half-filled with water, and a one thousand kip note (or any other note) is rolled up and placed into the hole. The 'boat' is a smoothened piece of foil with a small handle that is held between the index finger and the thumb, and it has a smooth surface for the candy to be melted on. The end of the one thousand kip note is placed over the melting candy so that the smoke can be inhaled by the user. The water is meant to filter it a bit, and it definitely gives it a smoother taste. The water makes noise when the user sucks the air through the gun. The candy leaves a black tar-like stain on the tinfoil so it is better to use a new boat for each candy. The safest way to dispose of the boat is to flush it down the toilet.

There was a knock on the door. Fon didn't move. To make sure it was Ting that had knocked on the door, and not the police, I opened the curtain slightly and peeked out the window into the hallway. Ting was standing there with a plastic bag in one hand and the keys to his motorbike in the other. He greeted me brightly when I opened the door. He walked passed me and sat across from Fon on the floor. He looked a bit shabby in sandals, light denim and a sleeveless Beer Lao T-shirt. It usually took people a few minutes to realize that he is gay. Ting had a pot-belly under the Beer Lao T-shirt, which suggested that, even though he was a dealer, he didn't smoke much candy. It is impossible to remain overweight while smoking candy for a long time. Ting was our dealer. Fon and I were loyal customers because we trusted him. He never made any problems for us and he always came when he said he would. Ting lived a strange lifestyle. He drove from guesthouse to guesthouse in and around falang town all day and night to deliver candy. Sometimes he made the deal and left straight away, but often he sat down and chatted away with his customers. He drank beer and played cards, and then when he got a call from a customer, he was gone again.

Ting took two bottles of Beer Lao, a packet of chewing gum and a bag of ice out of the plastic bag. Fon handed him a pair of scissors. He cut an empty bottle of water in half, threw in a handful of ice and filled it with beer.

"Here, Walt. Beer."

Ting placed the beer on the floor to his right, as a way of inviting me to join him. Originally I had wanted to sleep for the rest of the night, but now that there was candy involved, my plan quickly changed. I had bought hundreds of candies in the last few months and shared them with Fon, so I didn't want to miss a rare chance to be on the receiving end. Fon ripped up all the boats that she had made and threw them away.

"Why did you do that?" I asked.

"This foil is better," she answered, opening up the new packet of chewing gum that Ting had brought.

"Why you care?" Ting asked me. "You want to smoke fast? Wait a little."

"I can wait, but she takes too long making the boats."

"She just want to make perfect for you," Ting replied.

Bullshit! I thought to myself. *She doesn't give a shit about me. She is just hoping I get bored and go to sleep.*

"How many candies did you give Fon?" I asked Ting.

8

Ting looked at Fon and hesitated. "Why you ask me? Ask Fon. She right here."

"He give me five candies," Fon announced, irritated.

"You want buy more?" Ting asked me.

"No money."

"It's okay. You friend. I give you five more now and you pay me later."

"Not yet," I said, very tempted. "Maybe later."

Ting and Fon talked amongst themselves in Lao. I could understand bits and pieces of what they were saying, but basically I was just listening for names, place names and times. Ting took out a big wad of money and handed Fon a hundred thousand kip – about ten U.S. dollars. Ting and I made eye contact as he stuffed the rest of his money into his pocket.

"I give her loan. Don't worry," he said.

"Why do you need money?" I asked Fon.

I thought we were going to try to sleep soon.

"I just need," Fon replied, rubbing a long piece of foil with her thumb to make it smooth.

Fon sat closer to me and handed me the gun. She pulled her long brown hair behind her ears so that it wouldn't get in the way. She tested the flame of the lighter. The flame was too big, even when it was turned down to the minimum. A small flame is better when smoking candy because it allows the user to control how much of the pill they burn. If the flame is too big, it burns the pill too quickly and a lot of the smoke ends up bypassing the gun and rising up towards the ceiling. Fon handed the lighter to Ting – the expert. He ripped off the steel around the head of the lighter and hacked the settings. I'm not sure exactly how he did it, but he managed to make the flame the same size as a tiny drop of water.

With a tiny flame in hand, Fon signaled for me to get in position. I held the gun in position over the boat and she started to melt the candy very slowly. Barely any smoke was coming out. I waited patiently. She was leaning towards me so I could see that she wasn't wearing a bra. I could also see beads of sweat gathering on her upper lip. It was very hot in the room. I tapped her on the knee to signal her to stop.

"Why you stop?" she asked.

I exhaled, but only a tiny bit of smoke came out.

"There was no smoke. Just give it to me. I can do it."

"I do for you. Okay. One more time."

This time she burnt the candy a little bit quicker, but it still wasn't enough. Fon saw that I was annoyed.

"Slowly, slowly, Walt. You want to do too fast," Fon said.

"Yes, not good for your body," Ting added.

"I know, but she does it too slowly. There's barely any smoke."

Whenever we talked about candy, Fon talked to me like a parent talking to a child, or a teacher talking to a student. I had tried candy a couple of times before I met Fon, but basically I was a novice. I didn't know how to make a boat or a gun, and I had no idea which plastic bottles were good for making guns or which brand of chewing gum had good foil for making boats. Fon thought me all this. She also taught me to smoke slowly. At the start, I couldn't hold the lighter, the boat and the gun all at the same time, so I couldn't burn the candy for myself. Fon had to burn it for me. This gave her control. But after a few weeks, I got the knack of holding the boat up to my mouth with my knee, thus leaving one hand free for the lighter and the other hand free for the gun. I thought I would be in control of my own candy after this – especially considering I was the one paying for it all – but I was wrong. Fon still liked to control everything. Smoke slowly. Perfect boats. Make and remake guns over and over again until it lets out minimal sound. Smoke in the bathroom. Smoke in the living room. Turn on the fan. Turn on the air conditioner. Change the water in the gun. Some of her instructions were for the good of our health, others were for our safety, but some of her requests seemed completely random.

Fon was sick of my complaining so she gave me one of the pills to smoke by myself. I made my own boat and smoked the candy quickly. Ting left without saying goodbye to me. While I rested on the bed, Fon went into the bathroom for an hour and smoked the last two candies. I wondered what would happen that night. Why did Fon need the money? Why did she insist on getting more candy? Usually I am the one who pushes to get more candy. Fon is usually the one who wants to rest after a two or three day session, but not this time.

Fon came out of the bathroom fully clothed and with dry hair. She placed her money and her phone in her back pocket and started cleaning the apartment. There were beer bottles left over from Ting's visit, but there were also bits of toilet paper, empty plastic bottles, lighters and pieces of foil on the floor that Fon and I had left there during our four-day session. Fon threw everything into a plastic bag and said, "I'll throw this away outside. And I go to Don Chan. I come back later."
Don Chan is a night club in Vientiane.

"Fon, it's already two AM."

"I know. I just go for one beer and say hello my friends."

"But Don Chan closes at three o'clock."

"You no go, right? You say you want to sleep."

Fon didn't tell me in advance that she was going to Don Chan because she was worried that I would insist on joining her. There was a reason why she wanted to go alone. I guessed that she had agreed to

11

take a phone call from her sponsor that night at a certain time. I didn't know for certain that she had a sponsor, but she once told me that she had a friend in France who sometimes sent her money when she really needed it. According to Fon, they were never anything more than friends – he was just a really nice guy who helped her sometimes. But I guessed that he was Fon's sponsor. He probably came to Laos once a year for a week to see his 'girlfriend' (Fon), and for the rest of the year he probably sent her money every month. Every now and then I could see Fon making strange plans that were designed to give her some time on her own. For example, one night on the way home from Don Chan, her friend drove me fifteen minutes outside of the city. Apparently, he got lost and couldn't find my room. But I lived a ten-minute walk from Don Chan, and that friend had been to my room several times. It seemed bizarre to me at the time, but I can see now that it was all a plan to give Fon some time alone to take a phone call from her sponsor in France. This time I could see through Fon's plan, but I had no energy to stop her. If I suddenly jumped out of bed and said that I would go to Don Chan with her, she would probably just take the phone call in the toilets in Don Chan. Fon spent a lot of time in toilets.

Strangely enough, for the first few days of a session, when the candy is streaming through my blood, I have a great desire for women, but I cannot carry out the act well. It's a very unfortunate side effect of smoking candy. When I smoked candy the first few times, I smoked in moderation, so I didn't have this problem, but as my habit got worse, this side effect emerged. However, the good thing was that on the third and fourth day of the session, as I started to smoke less, as I started to rest and wait for sleep to come, my body felt exhausted but my desire for women became greater than ever and I become capable again. So, when

12

Fon said that she was going to Don Chan, I saw a golden opportunity to have a girl over.

I waited for a few minutes to make sure Fon had left. I walked out into the hallway and I even went as far as the front gate of the complex to make sure that her car was no longer there. I hurried back to my room and looked through the contacts in my phone. There were some names of real people in my phone book, but there were also a lot of initials and random nicknames to describe women that I knew. I couldn't write their real names because Fon looked through my phone sometimes. Some of the women were people she knew, and one of them was her best friend. The woman I messaged this time was not Fon's friend. Her name was Nit. She was eating noodles near the Bor Pen Nyang bar with her friends. When I told her that Fon had popped out for an hour, she said that she could come to my room in ten minutes. I was delighted. It had been a long time since I had been with Nit. It was difficult to make plans with these local women.

'I come in ten minutes,' Nit messaged me, but usually in this type of situation I would get another message from the woman thirty minutes later saying, 'I no have motorbike. I wait for my friend. I come in fifteen minutes. I promise.'

This time I only had about an hour to play with before Fon was due back from Don Chan, so I wanted to be very clear with Nit.

'Fon will come back in 50 minutes, so if you cannot come in the next ten minutes, don't come. We can meet next time.'

'I come ten minutes. I on friend bike now. We smoke?'

'No time to smoke, sorry. But I give you money. You can buy and smoke later with your friends.'

I was excited. It was difficult to hook up with Nit because she spent long spells with her family in her hometown, and sometimes she

13

went traveling around Laos and Thailand with her falang boyfriends. This time she had just come back from a couple of weeks in the south of Thailand with an Italian man. I had seen her the night before in Don Chan and she had given me her new number.

"I want smoke with you. We can go guesthouse. We can do like before. I no tell Fon," she said to me in Don Chan, while Fon was in the bathroom.

Nit messaged me to say that she had arrived. I went to the front gate and let her in. I waved to her friend, Nui, as she drove away on her bike. Nui was a friend of Fon's, but there was no danger of her ever telling Fon about this.

Nit was wearing a long red dress. She was a little heavier than most Lao women, but the advantage of this weight was that her breasts were also much bigger. Nit smoked regularly, but she only smoked one or two candies, and then she would sleep the next day. She never went a long time without eating or sleeping, so that's why she kept her weight. Nit also never drank more than one or two beers, so she was completely sober, even though she had been in Bor Pen Nyang all night hoping to find a falang.

When we got inside my room, I explained to Nit, "Fon went to Don Chan. But Don Chan closes at three o'clock. I think she will come here at about two-thirty. So let's do it quickly. If she comes back before we finish, you have to go out the back door and wait in the alley for five minutes. I will open the gate for Fon, bring her into the room, and after five minutes, you go out.

"But gate locked."

"I will leave the gate unlocked. But the most important thing is, when you go out the side way, you must wait in the alley for five minutes. Okay? Or else Fon will see you."

"Okay. First, I shower."

"No, it's okay. Let's just start," I said.

Nit hesitated. We looked at each other.

"Okay. Shower quickly," I said.

It occurred to me that Nit might have met a man in Bor Pen Nyang earlier in the night for 'short time'. 'Short time' was code for 'quick sex and then part ways'.

While Nit showered, I prepared a hundred thousand kip (ten dollars) for her. She could get twice as much for 'short time' with a tourist, but falangs who lived in Vientiane weren't expected to pay tourist rates.

"How much you smoke today?" Nit asked me when she climbed into bed. "You look tired."

"Today I smoked about ten, but the problem is this is my fourth day without sleep."

"Be careful. Don't go ding-dong like other falang in Laos. They smoke candy too long time and go crazy. You sweet man. I no want see you crazy. Already you lose weight too much."

"I'll be okay. Don't worry. We don't have much time."

It was exciting to be with Nit, but even in the act I felt regret that I was too pushed for time to fully enjoy the moment. There was an overview of passion without the time to appreciate the detail. And there was huge pressure to finish quickly – that's not easy to do on your fourth day without sleep. I started to feel tingling in my toes and fingers. I had experienced this feeling before. If I stop and wait a few minutes, the tingling feeling goes away. But I didn't have time to stop and wait. The feeling spread to my face. I felt my cheeks tingling. I kept going. I felt like I was close to the end so I didn't want to stop. I thought that if I stopped, I would need to take a few minutes to recover and start again, and then I might not have enough time to ejaculate before Fon came back. I kept

15

going, and then the tingling feeling that had spread from my hands to my cheeks was now in my toes, my ears and my nose. And then I froze! The tingling feeling shot through my whole body. My whole body, from head to toes, was suddenly paralyzed with intense pins and needles. I couldn't move an inch. This lasted twenty seconds or more. I was terrified. I had never felt anything like it before. I thought my heart had stopped. I expected the lights to go out at any moment. I didn't have any great moments of epiphany or enlightenment. To be honest, I didn't even think about my family or my life back home. I just thought how stupid I must look to Nit. *What must she think of me?* I thought. Nit pulled away from me in fright. She saw that I couldn't move. I stared at her. I wanted to ask for her help but I couldn't even move my mouth. I tried desperately to move my hands. My fists were clinched tightly together and I couldn't unclench them.

"Are you okay, Walt? Walt? What is it?"

My body was suddenly released from whatever had hold of it. My muscles relaxed. I sat on the side of the bed and I put both hands over my face. My eyes welled up with tears.

"Are you okay?" Nit asked again.

"Yes, give me one minute."

"You want some water?"

"No."

"You want go hospital?"

"No. That was weird. My whole body froze. I thought it was my heart."

"You smoke too much, Walt. You need sleep."

"I know."

We both got dressed and I gave Nit the money that I had counted out earlier.

"You go out the side way and wait in the alley. I will open the gate. If Fon is not there, I will call you and you can go. If Fon comes, you will have to wait in the alley until she comes into the room, okay?"

"Okay. Will you be okay?"

"Yes, I will be fine. I will sleep tonight. I promise."

Five minutes after Nit left, I heard Fon walking up the hallway towards my room. She was laughing and talking with someone. Usually it was quite fun when Fon brought her friends back to my room after Don Chan, especially when they were women, but this time I was furious that she brought people with her. She knew that I was exhausted. I opened the door for Fon before she had a chance to knock.

"I found your friend in Don Chan," she said.

A woman named On was standing next to Fon. I had only ever met On once before, a couple of months ago when I first hooked up with Fon. That night On came back to my room with me and Fon. We smoked until the morning and then a tuk-tuk driver came to pick up On because she had to go meet a Chinese business man. Back then On was incredibly beautiful. She was slim and she had beautiful dark skin, and long brown hair down to her shoulders. The few months since then had been harsh on her. She had become too skinny and she was missing one of her front teeth, yet she still looked good, which is a testament to her beauty. But I didn't understand why Fon referred to On as my 'friend'. On did not have a word of English, and the first time we met I couldn't speak much Lao, so we barely said anything to each other. But then Ted came into view – the 'friend' that Fon was referring to.

2

Ted was an English lad in his mid-thirties. He didn't live in Laos. He visited three or four times a year, and he stayed for a couple of weeks at a time. The last time I had met him, I gave him a loan of my hard drive so that he could put movies and TV shows onto his laptop. He didn't have a chance to meet me again before he left Laos, so he entrusted one of his Lao girlfriends to return it to me. A couple of days later, I got a call from an international number. It was Ted calling from Somalia. He gave me a quick call to make sure that I got my hard drive back. I didn't have anybody else around me in Vientiane who would be that considerate.

"Jesus! You look like shit, Walt"

That's how Ted greeted me.

"Really? But I lost weight and my skin is perfect," I replied.

"Yeah, you look like a fuckin' skeleton."

Ted and On sat on the sofa while Fon and I sat at the edge of the bed. I noticed some long black hairs on the floor. Nit's hair was much longer than Fon's, and it was much darker than On's hair. If Fon saw the long hairs she would suspect something.

"Who is gonna make the call?" Ted asked.

"Fon, can you call Ting?" I asked, subtly trying to gather some of the long black hairs with my feet and kick them under the bed.

"How many you want to order?" Fon asked.

"Enough to get us all fucked up!" Ted answered.

"How about me and you pay for ten each? And then we all share." "We can order more later if we need to," I suggested to Ted.

Ted agreed and On called Ting. I could have suggested buying thirty each and Ted would have agreed. This guy had no limits. He was an ex-British army soldier who started to work in private security when he left the army. He provided security for cargo ships along the African coast, because in that area cargo ships were frequently hijacked by Somali pirates. Ted often told me that he was earning ridiculous money, so he said whenever he had time off he was intent on living like a rock star. On spoke with Ting for a few minutes on the phone, and then she passed on the message to Fon in Lao.

"Ting come in two minutes. He in guesthouse near here," Fon translated for us.

Ted looked relieved that he wouldn't have to wait long before the candy came.

"Any fucking beer, lad?" he asked me.

"No beer," Fon replied for me. "You want to buy, Walt? On can message Ting and ask him to bring."

"Sure", I said. "Ask him to bring four beers."

On sent a message to Ting, and Fon started making boats from a sheet of foil that On had taken out of her bag.

"What happened to you anyway?" Ted asked me. "The last time I saw you, you barely even smoked candy. You didn't even know how. I had

19

to burn it for you and get the foil ready."

"I met Fon - that's what happened to me. This is my fourth day without sleep. I was planning on sleeping tonight, but then you came, so fuck it! You treated me to loads of candy last time so I'll get this one."

"No, let's pay for ten each like we agreed."

"No, I'll get it this time. How's your pregnant girlfriend anyway? Isn't she due soon?"

"Yeah, about that. She gave birth to a baby girl last night. I'm a dad," Ted said, with a big grin on his face.

I stood up and shook Ted's hand to congratulate him. I knew that he was excited about becoming a father.

"Yeah, let's celebrate," Ted said, shaking my hand firmly.

Ted's girlfriend was a Thai woman who lived in the Thai city Nong Khai, which is near the Laos–Thailand border. I knew that Ted was not allowed into Thailand because of a conviction a few years ago, so I was careful not to ask about when he would go to see his newborn baby. I told Fon about Ted's good news. She congratulated him warmly and then translated the news for On. On gave him a thumbs-up and said, "Good."

It was a weird situation because I knew that the plan was for Ted to take On back to his hotel room after we all smoked.

Ting was delayed a few minutes because he had to stop off at a store to buy beer. When he came, he sat down on the floor with On, and Ting started showing her all the candy he had brought with him. He had about fifty pink pills in a small plastic bag, and then a couple packs of ten pills separated into tiny plastic zip bags. He placed two packs of ten in front of On, and then they both started looking through the big bag.

"What are you looking for?" I asked Ting.

"On wants to do a green candy," Ting replied.

I had only ever seen pink candies. I turned to Fon and asked, "What do the green ones do?"

"They make you relax and calm. You want?"

"Okay. Get one for each of us."

We gave Ting the money for twenty four candies. He stayed with us and drank some beer, but he didn't smoke. Ting made an effort to be particularly nice to Ted. From how anxious Ted was to start smoking and by how quickly he smoked, Ting could see that Ted would be a good customer to have. After Ted smoked three candies within ten minutes, Ting said to him, "Now drink some beer and rest for twenty minutes. I make nice boat for you and give you two candies for free."

We had started with twenty four candies, but that number soon halved. Fon and I smoked slowly because we were coming to the end of a long session. In contrast, Ted was smoking for the first time in a couple of months, so he was devouring them as quickly as he could. On put a couple of candies onto one boat every time, then she turned her body away from the group and smoked them within a couple of minutes. She looked like an expert. Soon Fon let me know that there were only five candies left, and four of them were green candies. In this type of situation it's impossible to keep track of all the candies. Fon could easily have snuck a couple into her handbag to keep for another day. She also had the habit of putting a candy on a boat, melting it a small bit, and then hiding the boat in her bag so that she could smoke it later on her own, probably in the toilet.

"I'm not bothered with the green ones," Ted said. "Just change them for the normal ones."

On, Fon and I kept a green candy each, and Ting changed Ted's green candy for a pink one to make him happy.

"You want buy more?" Ting asked Ted.

"Sure. Give me ten more."

Then Ted suddenly asked about ice.

"Ice very expensive in Laos. Much more expensive than candy."

"Do you have any?" Ted asked.

"My friend have. I can call him. You want?"

"How much?"

Ting turned to On and Fon, and he asked them about the price of ice. They seemed pleasantly surprised that Ted was interested in buying ice.

"On said it's about 600,000 for ice... for a gram," Fon said. "But you don't have the glass pipe to smoke it."

"It's okay. I can make a boat and put it on that, same as candy."

Fon translated Ted's words into Lao. Both On and Ting disagreed strongly.

"No, no," Ting said. "You cannot smoke ice on boat. Must be very small ice in small glass pipe. Ice very strong so boat is not good. No, no. I ask my friend if he can give glass pipe."

Ting called his friend. Ted made a boat in the meantime. It turned out quite badly, so On ripped it up and made a new one for him.

"My friend have candy and glass pipe. 600,000 for ice but you buy glass pipe, 300,000."

Ted thought for a few minutes. I tried to talk Ted out of it. It seemed like a waste of money to buy a glass pipe for thirty dollars and only use it once.

"Is the pipe useful to you at all?" Ted asked me.

"No," I replied, "absolutely not. And I wouldn't keep it in my room either in case somebody found it."

There was no point reasoning with him. It wasn't a lot of money to him, so he went ahead with the order. Ting took the money from Ted, and he left straight away to make the pick-up.

I lay on the bed, but I continued talking with Ted. Fon and On sat together on the floor, making boats and chatting together in Lao. Since Ted had come, I had only smoked one candy, and I had only smoked that one because I didn't want my friend to feel awkward. I placed my index finger and middle finger on my wrist and checked my heart beat. Compared to earlier in the night, it had settled down a lot. It was still quite fast and faint, but I couldn't feel any missed beats. My body had plenty of energy because of the candy, but my head felt empty and I felt on edge. I was fiddling with my hair one minute and biting my nails the next. My hands wouldn't stay still.

"You can keep the pipe if you want, or sell it to someone," Ted said. "I'm off to Thailand tomorrow night."

"What? You told me before that you are not allowed into Thailand."

"Yeah, did I tell you the story? I was playing poker with a load of Thai guys in a hotel room in Pattaya. The police raided the room and found a shit load of ice and candy, and of course everybody blamed the falang. I was in the Bangkok Hilton for a month."

"The Bangkok Hilton? The hotel?"

"No, not the fucking hotel. It's the notorious prison in Bangkok. It's a fucking shithole. There are some documentaries about it online. You should check them out. Didn't I tell you this story last time?"

"Yeah, you did, but you didn't mention the prison part. I thought you were just deported and banned from entering again."

"Well, I am barred from entering."

"But you are going tomorrow night."

"Yeah, there's no way I'm gonna let them stop me from seeing my baby."

"So how will you get in?"

"I've paid a guy to bring me cross the river in a small boat in the middle of the night. It's all arranged."

"That sounds really dodgy. What if you get caught?"

"Fuck it. It will be okay."

Ting came back quickly with a small bag of ice. I had only ever smoked ice once in Bangkok, and the gram of ice I got was definitely bigger than this one.

"Are you sure that is a gram?" I asked Ting.

"I don't know ice much. My friend say it's a gram," Ting replied.

Ted didn't care about the quantity. He inspected the pipe and he was happy that it looked clean and new. He tried to pour some of the ice into the glass pipe, but it looked like some of the ice would fall onto the ground, so On insisted on doing it for him.

I took one smoke off the ice, but after that I didn't touch it because I wanted to leave it for Ted. He had spent almost a hundred dollars on the pipe and the gram - that is a lot of money in Laos. I didn't feel comfortable smoking it. But On and Fon didn't care how much it cost, especially On. She went through the ice as quickly as Ted had gone through the candy. And On insisted on burning the ice when it was Ted's turn to smoke.

"I take care of you." she kept saying.

"Let On take care you. She want. She like you," Ting added.

Did she really want to take care of him or did she just want to control the amount he smoked? When Fon burned candy for me, she often put the flame under the part of the boat that didn't have much candy on it so that I wouldn't get much smoke. But then when it was her turn, she put the flame under the part of the boat that had the most candy so that she got the most smoke. It took me nearly a month of smoking candy before I figured this out. Fon did it in a very subtle way. I guess On was playing the same trick on Ted because after a while he took the bag of ice, put the biggest remaining crystal of ice into the pipe and burned it by himself. On wasn't very happy with this, so she turned away from the group and played on her phone for a while. Fon and Ting said a few things to her in Lao – it sounded like advice – and she eventually returned to the group.

The ice didn't last long. Ted thought about whether he should buy another gram or not, but it was already 6 AM and we all needed a break from smoking. Even On didn't show any interest in smoking more ice. She smoked a couple of green candies with Fon instead. I smoked my green candy too, but it didn't have the calming affect that I had hoped for.

"I smoke this and then sleep," Fon said.

Finally, my chance to get some sleep was coming. I made a boat for my candy and smoked it slowly, while Ted was thinking about what to do next. On made a boat for him and placed two candies on it, but Ted placed it on top of the empty bag of ice and left it there for a while.

"What you do now?" Ting asked Ted.

"I don't know," he replied, and then he turned to me.

"I'm on my last legs, man," I said. "I need to sleep, and then maybe I can meet you for a beer tonight in Samlo Pub. You can take On back to your place. She seems interested."

Ting agreed.

"On is my little sister," he said. "She like family. We know each other long time. She take good care of man."

Ting seemed much closer to On than he was to Fon, and this was good news for me because it meant that I could contact On through Ting in the future. He had brought me girls several times in the previous few months behind Fon's back. On didn't speak English and she didn't go to any of the falang bars, so I never held much hope of hooking up with her before. I met her the odd time in Don Chan, but I was always with Fon. But now I could see a clear path from me to beautiful On.

Ting got a call from a customer. He had to go make a drop off. He told Ted to call him if he needed any more ice or candy. Fon went for a shower while On rested on the bed alone. As soon as Fon turned on the shower, Ted whispered to me, "What the fuck happened to you man? How did you end up like this?"

"What do you mean? You smoke more than I do."

I knew that Ted wasn't trying to argue with me or look down on me. He seemed genuinely concerned.

"But I smoke for a few weeks and then fuck off and work for a couple of months. You are pale as shit. It looks like you haven't seen the sun in months."

"Yeah, I hate going out during the day when I smoke."

"So you stay inside and buy her candy all day? She's taking you for a ride. You need to wake up, man."

"I know. I do spend a lot on candy for us, but fuck it. I have a flight booked home for the end of August, and then I'll never come back here again, so I might as well just enjoy it while I'm here."

"But are you enjoying it, stuck in here with her all the time? Man, why are you staying with one woman the whole time? And she's not even that hot. Remember when we used to drink in Samlo together? You used to have women coming up to you all the time, even if you were a bit fucking chubby. But now you stick with her, and she leaves you in here while she fucks off to Don Chan on her own."

"You don't know what you're talking about. What if I told you that just before you came here tonight, a woman was here and she left through the back door only minutes before you came here with Fon and On."

"Really?"

"Yes. And sometimes I go to a guesthouse up the road to meet girls for short time. I've plenty going on."

"Okay. Then it's not as bad as I thought," Ted said. "But it looks like you're stuck in a rut. You need to get out more. Come to Samlo tonight for a few beers before I cross over to Thailand."

"I'll try. But I really need sleep. Four nights with no sleep, and when the woman came tonight I had a kind of episode during it. I don't know if it was a heart attack or what, but my whole body seized up and I couldn't move. And my heartbeat is really irregular sometimes. Sometimes when my heart is beating fast, it suddenly stops and there is a full second before the next beat."

I expected some concern or advice from Ted, but all he said was, "You're fucking paranoid lad."

When Fon came out of the shower, she said, "Let's go! I take Ted and Fon to Ted's hotel."

"I'll go too. Let me brush my teeth first," I said.

"You don't need to come, Walt," Fon said. "It's not far. I come back soon. Don't worry."

In truth, I didn't want to go, but I imagined what would happen

28

if I didn't go. Fon would come back five hours later and I would be left imagining the worst. I held up the glass pipe and asked if anybody wanted it. Fon translated my question into Lao and On stepped forward. She wrapped up the glass pipe in tissue and placed it carefully into her bag.

There were seven candies left. Usually in this situation, Fon would put them into her bag and carry them, but on this occasion she said that she was sick of being the one who carried the candies all the time.

"You carry them, Walt, or Ted carry them. They are his candies," Fon suggested, standing at the door, with her car keys in her hand.

"But I don't want to smoke anymore," I replied. "I don't want to carry them. How about On?"

"She is carrying the pipe already," Fon argued. "She can't carry the candies too."

"Just throw them away," Ted said. "We can order more when we get to the hotel."

"But it's such a waste to throw them away," I said.

The problem was that if I carried the candies, I had nowhere to hide them, except in my wallet or my pocket – not exactly good hiding places. I tried to think of a better place to hide them.

"Let's go!" Fon said again, with On and Ted standing either side of her at the door.

I remembered that I had a small hole in the back of one of my sneakers. I wrapped up the candies tightly in a small plastic bag and stuck them into the hole. They fitted perfectly. Surely, even if I was searched by the police, they wouldn't find anything.

Ted's hotel was alongside the Culture Hall, right in the heart of the falang area. It was still dark outside but the sun was on its way. On our way into falang town we passed the President's house. He must have been still asleep, because all the lights were off. Before I started smoking candies, I used to walk along this area every evening, listening to music and trying to think of stories to write. When I got back to my room I would write for an hour or two, and then go to Noi's Restaurant for dinner, before going to Samlo for a few beers and a game of pool. My life was very different back then.

When we came to the tourist downtown area, I saw a few ladyboys that I knew. They were standing on the street corner across from Khop Chai Deu restaurant. Ladyboys waited at this corner every night and propositioned falangs passing by. A motorbike pulled up in front of them and took the two ladyboys back in the direction of my room.

"Is that Ting on the bike?" I asked Fon.

"Yes. Those ladyboys are his friends. You know them? Noy and Kip."

"Yes, I know them from Samlo."

As we drove a little further up the road, we saw monks in orange shawls walking towards us with a woven rice container in hand. The monk in the front was ringing a bell to let people know that they were coming. They were walking quite slowly along the side of the road, in a single line about fifteen monks long. I had seen this scene before. The monks walk along the streets at this time every morning, and Lao people, usually older women, sit alongside the road with a pile of rice or other food, and they each put a handful of food into the monks' rice container. The ladyboys had also seen this scene before – it was a custom in every town and city in Laos. The ladyboys respected the custom too much to stick around and sell sex on the street corner as the monks passed by.

"Do you know where Ted's hotel is?" I asked Fon.

"Yes, it's on the next right," she replied.

Of course she knew the hotel. I'm sure she knew every hotel in falang town. I had only ever stayed in the cheapest guesthouses in Vientiane. Those kinds of guesthouses didn't have an air conditioner or a TV in the cheap rooms. From the outside, Ted's hotel looked like luxury compared to the places I used to stay in. Fon parked across from the hotel. I checked my shoe to make sure the candies were still there. They were still packed into the hole tightly. Fon unfastened her seatbelt and checked her hair in the mirror.

"I thought we were going straight back to our room," I said as nicely as I could so as to not offend Ted.

"Let's just go in for a few minutes," Fon said.

We were all welcomed at reception by a beautiful Lao woman in a purple uniform, with her hair tied up nicely like an air stewardess.

"I have to get my room key," Ted told me.

I wanted to get up to the room as quickly as possible because I couldn't feel comfortable with the bag of candies stuck in the hole of my shoe.

"What's your room number?" the woman at reception asked Ted.

"Room number? God knows. I only checked in last night, and when I went out, I left my key at the reception. I can't remember the room number."

"No problem, sir," the woman said, turning to the computer screen. "What's your name?"

"Ken Jacobs."

Was Ted so fucked up on candy and ice that he couldn't even remember his name? Or was he using a fake name on purpose?

"Why did you give the name Ken Jacobs?" I asked Ted, as we followed him up the stairs.

"Sshh! I'll tell you when we get to our room."

As soon as Ted closed the door of his room, Fon and On dropped their handbags on the floor and sat on the bed. It was a nice room. The bed was huge and it was covered in lovely thick bedding. There was a TV sitting on top of a beautiful dark mahogany cabinet. In the corner by the bed there was a large armchair, and alongside the mahogany cabinet there was a small round table with a couple of wooden chairs. However, the thing that gave the room a sense of luxury was the thick purple carpet. Floors in Laos were always either tiled or wooden, so I had never stepped on or even seen carpet during my time in Laos.

"How much is this room?" I asked Ted.

"300,000 a night."

I thought that was crazy money. I couldn't imagine spending that much on a room for a night in Laos. It seemed like such a waste of money. When I used to stay in a guesthouse in falang town, I paid 50,000 kip a night. It didn't have an air conditioner, a TV or even a mattress with springs, but it was enough for me. I didn't bother sharing these thoughts with Ted because we had different ideas about these kinds of things. His pockets were far deeper than mine. I bent down to get the candies out of my shoe.

"Fuck!" I exclaimed.

The candies were gone, but nobody seemed to notice my sense of panic.

"We have a problem," I said, but of course only Ted and Fon could understand.

"The candies?" Ted asked, sounding annoyed. "I fucking knew it. What a stupid fucking place to hide them."

I checked my shoes again, but the candies were definitely gone. Fon told On about what had happened. She lay down on the bed without a care in the world.

"Where did you see them last?" Fon asked me.

"In the car, when we arrived. They were definitely in my shoe when I stepped out of the car."

"Let's just forget about them," Fon suggested.

"No, we won't just fucking forget about them!" Ted erupted. "What if someone in the hotel finds them. It will end up coming back to me."

We discussed who should go looking for the candies. I didn't want to go alone because I didn't want to leave Fon, On and Ted alone together. Ted didn't want to come with me because he didn't want to leave the two girls alone with all his stuff. And it would look weird if we all went out together. After a few minutes of arguing, Fon finally agreed to come with me to her car. As we walked down the hall, down the stairs and through the reception area, we scanned the floor for the small bag. We pretended that Fon wanted to get something from the trunk of her car, and while she was pretending to look for something in the trunk, I pretended to wait for her alongside the passenger door. But what I was actually doing was scanning the ground. We walked very slowly back to the hotel. On the way, I pretended to tie my shoe laces. In the reception, Fon inquired about the price of a room for one night, and then she tried to haggle for a discount, all in an attempt to buy me some time to look around the reception area. We walked up the stairs slowly, heads down, looking carefully at the carpet on each step. Nothing.

"So, now we are fucked!" Ted started to panic when I told him we couldn't find the candy. "We can't even order any more candy, because if your bag of candy is found and the police come, we sure as shit better not be smoking any in the room. And when you guys leave later, I'll be the one still here in my room until tonight."

"Maybe you should check out early and go to another hotel," I suggested.

"But this hotel has my name and passport details."

"Isn't it your fake name?"

"No, Ted is my fake name. Did you really think Ted Bundy was my real name?"

"That's what you introduced yourself as."

"That's just the name I use over here sometimes."

"Fuck! What do we do now?" I asked everybody.

Fon lay on the bed alongside On. Ted (I decided to keep calling him 'Ted') used the bathroom. The door opened outwards, and when he opened the door I noticed that the door pushed something along the carpet. It was the bag of candies. It must have fallen out of my shoe when I came into the room. Ted and I breathed a sigh of relief. Fon seemed annoyed, and On seemed removed from everything. Ted gave me a hard time for a few minutes.

"Who hides that shit in their shoe? No, who hides that shit in the outside of their shoe?" he repeated a couple of times, laughing.

"I need to smoke," I said, sitting down on one of the wooden chairs in the corner of the room. "I'll make a gun. Do you have any empty bottles of water or coke?"

"No, I just got here last night," Ted said, scanning the room from side to side for a solution.

I checked the trashcan under the table. It was completely empty.

"Is that a mini fridge under the TV?" I asked.

Bingo! I took a bottle of water from the fridge and borrowed Ted's lighter.

"Walt, I make the gun for you. Give me the bottle," Fon offered.

"No, it's okay. I'll make it quickly. You will take thirty minutes to make it."

Fon wasn't pleased with this remark.

We all took a drink from the bottle and then I poured the rest of the water down the sink. I removed the plastic packaging from the bottle, and with a small flame I made a small hole near the top of the bottle. I took a hotel pen from the table and used it to expand the hole and make it perfectly circular. I took a thousand kip note from my wallet and rolled it up like a cigarette. It took a minute or two to get it long enough and to make it the right width so that it would fit the hole tightly. Then I made sure that the one thousand kip note was pointing down into the bottle at a forty five degree angle. I held the bottle under the tap in the bathroom, and I put in enough water so that the end of the note was submerged in the water. I had finished making the boat in about three minutes.

"See. Easy," I said proudly.

I inhaled through the gun to make sure it worked properly.

"That's so loud, Walt," Fon said. "People in the hallway hear you when you smoke. Throw it away and I make another one."

I admit that it was loud, but I just wanted to smoke quickly and go home.

"It's fine," I said. "We can turn on the TV to cover the sound."

"It's too much. Throw it away. I make new one."

Fon took a bottle of coke from the fridge and started making her own boat in the opposite corner of the room.

Ted and I each smoked a candy very quickly, but after that we slowed down a lot. On lay on the bed with her eyes closed. Having seen the amount of ice and candy that she had smoked, I knew that she was not sleeping.

Ted noticed me looking at his suitcase under the bed. It was open just enough for me to see a colorful box and something fluffy inside.

"You want to see?" he asked.

He dragged the suitcase out from under the bed. He lifted up a pink teddy bear and a beautiful, soft comfort blanket. "I brought these for the little one," he said.

"And what about those?" I asked, pointing at the box of chocolates resting on top of his clothes in the suitcase.

"Those are for the girlfriend. She deserves a present too. I tell ya, it's fucking scary. I don't know if I can be a good dad. The life I've led for the last ten years doesn't suit fatherhood."

"But you can change your life," I said.

"You know, since I joined the army, I can't even hang around with civilians anymore. When I used to go back to my home in England and meet my old mates, I used to be fucking bored shitless. The shit they were talking about! We couldn't relate to each other anymore. I don't know if I could ever have that type of life."

"But I'm a civilian, and we hang out and get along well."

"Yeah, but we are in Laos and you are up for anything. It's not like being in a bar back in England talking about money problems and jobs. Fuck, when my mates used to talk about that shit, it bored me senseless."

Ted took a smoke from the gun. I flicked through the TV channels to see if this fancy hotel had any English channels other than CNN and BBC. I couldn't find anything interesting, so I left on the music channel – mostly Kpop was playing.

"And I can be a nasty fucker too!" Ted added.

He walked to the bathroom to throw the used boat down the toilet.

"What do you mean?" I asked him.

Ted came out from the bathroom and wiped his feet on the carpet.

"One time I was in a bar in Pattaya, and the owner of the bar was a falang – an English guy. I wanted to take one of the girls so I agreed to pay the barfine, but when he handed me the bill it included all the drinks that the girl had drank that night. But I had only arrived in the bar about an hour before closing time. I told him I'm not fucking paying for all her drinks. He started acting like a right prick and he was speaking shit. He was trying to look like mister big cock in front of all the women. I was done with him, so I whacked my lighter off of the counter, poured the lighter fluid all over him and lit him on fire."

Whenever Ted spoke about the army, his martial arts training in South Africa, and his job as security in Somalia, I always believed him. He seemed like a very genuine guy. Some of his stories were amazing to me, but he always explained things that happened in his life in a very matter-of-fact way. It never came across as bragging. However, when he told me this story about lighting a falang on fire in Pattaya, I didn't believe him for a second.

"But how could you have lit him on fire if you had already poured the lighter fluid over him?" I asked.

38

"I guess a tiny bit of fluid was left in the small tube, enough to make one last flame anyway. What kind of father will I be if I'm capable of that?"

Fon sat at the edge of the bed and started to smoke from her new gun. It sounded every bit as loud as mine. She handed Ted the gun and she asked him to try it. I noticed a big, black pair of headphones in Ted's bag.

"Try them on," he said, after he took a smoke from Fon's gun.

"What are they?"

"Sound proof headgear for gunfire."

I tried them on. They blocked out external sounds completely, leaving only the sound of my racing heartbeat to torment me. It reminded me of the incident with my heart six hours previous. I could see that Ted and Fon were saying something to each other, so I took off the headgear quickly.

Ted took a smart phone out from under his clothes in the suitcase. He used the hotel phone to call reception for the wifi password. Wifi wasn't common in Vientiane at the time. Only a couple of expensive cafes near Namphu Fountain and some high-end hotels offered this luxury. Before I started smoking candy I used to go to an internet café nearly every day. I would read up on the latest soccer news, listen to music on Youtube and sometimes play chess online. And, of course, I would email my family and some friends. When I started smoking candy, all that stopped. I started to stay in my room all day, and I only went out after midnight for a couple of beers in Don Chan.

Ted handed me the phone and told me to check my email or browse online if I wanted to. I hadn't checked my email in a couple of weeks, so that's the first thing I did. I read an email from my dad about how he was now working only two or three days a week, but with only him and my mom left in the house it was enough money to keep them going. Candy messes up your emotions when you smoke it too much, or perhaps it is just the lack of sleep. It makes you cold to some things and more sensitive to other things. An email like that from my dad usually wouldn't affect me much, but this time it brought a tear to my eye. I opened up to Ted about how I missed my parents, and how I felt sorry for them for having a son who ran away to the other side of the world and ended up smoking candy, wasting his life and money away.

"But it's only until August, and then I'll be away from all this shit," I told him again.

There was only one candy left. It rested on a piece of tissue in the middle of the table.

"Do you want to check your email, Fon?" I asked, holding out Ted's phone.

Fon looked away from me without answering. I repeated the question.

"On this phone?" she asked, suddenly annoyed.

"Yeah, why not? It has wifi. You can check your email or look at some websites."

"You'd love me to check my email wouldn't you?" she said, really pissed off.

"What does that mean?"

"I'm not stupid!"

Fon went into the bathroom. I was embarrassed that Ted had seen Fon and I have that weird argument. I didn't even know what the argument was about. When she came out of the bathroom she started gathering her things and cleaning up. She took a scissors from her bag (she always brought that type of thing around with her just in case) and cut up the gun that I had made.

"I leave this gun here for you and On," she said, referring to the gun that she had made, "but when you finish, cut or burn bottle so there no hole. Walt, I go back to room now. You stay here with your friend, no problem."

I said goodbye to Ted and I promised him that I would try to meet him that night for a beer in Samlo. On was still pretending to be asleep, but I knew she would wake up as soon as Fon and I left.

During the car ride back to my place, Fon explained why she had become so angry in Ted's room.

"I know why you want me to check my email. You want me put in name and password. Gmail and Yahoo keep password for long time, so you can see on your friend phone anytime. You want see my email. I know. I know. But I'm not stupid, Walt. I can't believe you! How can you and your friend try trick me like that?"

"I never even thought about that. I just thought you might want to use the internet. I never thought about saving your password and checking your email later. Why the fuck would I do that?"

"Because you want to know everything. You no trust me."

I didn't reply and Fon didn't add anything.

It took us a few minutes longer than usual to drive back to my place from falang town because the traffic was quite heavy at the three-way intersection in front of the President's House. Vientiane was a very tranquil, small and quiet city. There weren't any taxis or buses, and not many people could afford motorbikes, never mind cars, so the traffic in Vientiane was almost always very light. However, for about an hour in the morning and an hour in the evening the traffic on the main roads did tend to get heavy. I could never understand where all these people were going to or what kind of jobs they had? I mean, Laos was such a poor country, yet all these cars in the morning and evening suggested that there were a lot of professionals working in companies in Vientiane, but where? I guess the problem was that all I knew about Laos were cheap guesthouses, cheap restaurants, falang bars and candy. I had lived in Laos for nearly a year in total, but I had seen very little of the country and knew very little about its culture or its people. Even before I met Fon, my view of Vientiane was very limited. I lived in falang town for about eight months and visited the same restaurant and the same bar every single day. I only ever left falang town once a month because I had to do a visa run to Thailand. Those visa runs were a pain in the ass, but they were relatively short. I literally went to the Thai-Laos border in the morning, got stamped out of Laos on my passport, got stamped into Thailand, and then crossed the road and got stamped out of Thailand and then lined up to pay for a new Laos tourist visa. It was a pain because I usually had to wait over half an hour for the Laos visa, but I was back in falang town before noon.

When we got back to my room, I brushed my teeth and went straight into bed. Fon started cleaning the room and she arranged our things neatly. I was glad to be in bed at last. I tried to count the number of hours that it had been since I had last slept, but I couldn't figure it out exactly. All I knew was that I had been awake for nearly one hundred hours. I had only eaten two small meals during that time, and both times I had to force myself to lift up the spoon and put the rice into my mouth. Out of all the people that I knew who smoked candy, I was the only one who cared about trying to keep on weight and keep hydrated. I used to constantly drink water during the day and night, but it did little good because the caffeine in the candy made me pee everything out as soon as I drank it.

When you smoke candy, it completely kills your appetite. The last thing you want to do is eat. Candy makes your mouth and throat dry, so it takes a lot of effort to swallow anything solid. Plus, you can't taste the food, so eating food during a candy session is a very unpleasant experience. I often drank a couple of bottles of Beer Lao during the day or at night with Fon and our friends, so that gave my body a certain amount of calories, but it wasn't enough. I was losing too much weight. To intake more calories, I drank a bottle of milk every day, and I often went to a nearby bakery to buy a small birthday cake. It was a very cheap bakery. A small birthday cake only cost a couple of dollars, and it was covered with a layer of cream so it was very easy to swallow. There were some weeks when I ate a whole birthday cake by myself every day. It was my way of trying to keep on weight, but it didn't work. The weight continued to fall off me. Although I tried to care for my health in some ways, the one thing that I could not control was sleep. The lack of sleep was making me more and more agitated and more irascible. My left eye started to twitch sometimes when I spoke, and my hands were becoming increasingly restless. Even when I lay in bed, I would twirl my hair around and around with my fingers. If I was sitting on a chair, I would inevitably end up biting my nails or rubbing the stubble on my face with the palm of my hands over and over again.

Fon took a shower. I sat up on the edge of the bed for a few minutes to drink some water. I noticed a red dot on my left wrist. The red mark was on a vein, on the part of the wrist where you would place your two fingers to check your pulse. A narrow red line had stretched from the red mark to half way up my arm. I looked at it closely for a few minutes to see if the line was still moving up my arm or whether it had stopped. I couldn't tell either way. I tried to see if the red line was following one of my veins, but my body was so weak that I could only see the blue of my veins at my wrist. The red line wasn't straight or particularly curved; it just looked like the track of a vein. I started to panic. The conclusion that I came to was that there was some kind of blockage in my vein, and whatever was causing that blockage was making its way up my arm, towards my heart. I used a pen to mark how far the line had progressed up my arm. I lay in bed and waited five minutes. When I looked at my arm again, I could clearly see that the red line had stretched a couple of centimeters past the pen mark. I checked my pulse. It was fast and faint. I could barely detect it with my two fingers. The only thing I could do was rest and hope that my heartbeat slowed down.

Fon came out of the shower and sat next to me at the edge of the bed. She took two used boats out from her bag.

"There is some candy left on these boats. We can smoke one each and then go."

"Go where?" I asked.

I feared Fon's reply.

"To my house. It is my brother's birthday today."

"Which brother?"

"Somphone"

"Fon, I haven't slept in a long time. I just want to sleep today, please."

"Me too, but it's my brother's birthday. We need to go. I tell them you come already."

"Why did you tell them that? I never said that I will go."

"You did. Yesterday you said you go."

"No, I didn't. Anyway, I'm exhausted. This time I really can't go. Look at my arm."

I showed Fon my arm and explained to her what I thought the problem was.

"You always worry about your heart. Why you smoke candy if you worry about your heart? Why you no stop?"

"That kind of talk isn't really helpful right now. I need to know what to do with this red line. What if it keeps going up to my shoulder and over to my heart?"

"We can go to my house and you can rest there. No candy in my house. We can sleep tonight and stay there for few days to get away from candy."

"Yes, I want to go, but not right now."

Of course I wanted to go to Fon's family home for her brother's birthday. Her family had always been incredibly kind to me. Only a few weeks after Fon and I hooked up, Fon didn't feel well so she went home to rest. Her family brought her to the doctor the next day and she was diagnosed with Denghi fever. When Fon called me to let me know she was in hospital, I told Fon that I also felt weak and that I had a fever and a headache. Fon sent her friend, Guy, to collect me straight away. Guy brought me to the hospital on the back of his scooter. I was also diagnosed with Denghi fever. Fon and I were in hospital for three nights and Fon's mom stayed with us the whole time. Fon said that her mom wanted to take care of me because I was so far away from my own mom. I always felt close to Fon's mom after that.

Fon and I sat in silence for a while. She wanted to see if I would change my mind about going to her home for Somphone's birthday, but eventually she gave up. Fon smoked the two boats and then left. She said that she would come back to collect me and bring me to her home that night. I was glad to be alone. I turned off the light, turned on the air conditioner and hid under the bed clothes. Finally, I got some sleep.

3

I woke up that night at eight o'clock. I could have fallen straight back to sleep but I wanted to get up and eat something first. I checked my arm. Thank God, the dot and the line on my arm had completely gone. I wasn't sure whether to be grateful for a lucky escape or to feel foolish for being so paranoid. I had two messages on my phone. One of the messages was from Fon, saying that I didn't need to come to her home that night and that I should sleep. The other message was from my friend, Keith. It simply read 'I am back!'

Keith was an English lad around the same age as me, mid-twenties. He usually worked in England for a few months to save up money, and then he came to Laos and stayed as long as he could before his money ran out. This time, however, he had only been home for about three weeks. He wasn't due back in Laos until the end of the summer, so I was surprised to see his message. I replied to Keith to ask him about his plans for the night, and then I called Noi's Restaurant to order food. I ordered two green curries and two steaks. It amounted to about ten dollars. I wouldn't be able to eat all that food that night, but I thought it would be handy to have food in the apartment in case I got hungry. After I ordered food, Keith replied and told me to meet him at Samlo later. A part of me wanted to ignore Keith's message. I needed to eat, rehydrate and then go back to bed. But the other part of me was happy to have a chance to go out and party with my friend, without Fon. I wanted to call Ting to order candy, but I was worried that Ting would come before the food was delivered. If that happened, I might end up smoking candy first, and then I wouldn't be able to eat anything. The smart move was to wait until the food was delivered and then call Ting. While I was waiting for the food, I popped out to the supermarket near my apartment. It was nice to walk along the street and breathe in some fresh air. I could breathe in deep, full breaths without worrying about my heartbeat. It was nice to not be sweating. It was nice to feel calm and relaxed for the first time in a long time. I felt thankful to be hungry and thirsty. In the market I bought a bag of ice and a two liter bottle of cola. I don't know what my body was telling me, but whenever I was recovering from a hard session on candy, my body craved cola. Half of the bottle was gone by the time I got back to my apartment.

As soon as the food was delivered, I called Ting. He was in a guesthouse nearby, so he was able to get to my place before I could finish my meal. He sat next to me on the sofa and took out the ten candies that I had ordered.

Ting took out a lighter and said, "I make a small flame for you. I know you cannot do. This my present to you."

I paid Ting 220,000 kip for the ten candies.

"You smoke ten candies alone?" Ting asked.

I didn't know how to reply to this question. My plan was to smoke five candies and then hide five candies somewhere before I went out, but I didn't want Ting to know that I planned to hide drugs in my apartment.

"I smoke five. I don't know about the other five," I replied, as vaguely as I could.

"What you do tonight?" Ting asked me.

"I go Samlo. Keith is back."

"Who Keith?"

"You know Keith. He is the English guy with blond hair. He was best friends with Dan. He dated Ning before."

"Oh, yes. I know Keith. He crazy boy."

"Why you think he is crazy?"

"Everyone know he crazy. Be careful him. He smoke too much."

"But I smoke too much too."

"But you not crazy....yet," Ting said, and we both laughed.

"If he needs candy, can I give him your number?"

"Yes, I give him good price."

"How much?"

"Same you. Ten for 220,000. Good price," Ting said, putting the lighter back together.

Ting tested the flame. It was tiny. Next, he took out foil from his pocket and started making a boat for me.

"Is 220,000 really a good price?" I asked him. "Honestly?"

"Yes. Good price. Why not?"

"But I buy about 30 candies from you every day. I must be your best customer. But I think you give Lao people a better price. Maybe

200,000 for ten, or even less, right?"

"Usually, falang pay 300,000 or 400,000 for ten. You only pay 220,000 because you friend. You pay Lao people price. Same same."

I didn't believe him, but I didn't want to argue. Ting never made any problem for me, and he never told Fon about all the women I met. Plus, he sometimes gave me a couple of candies for free and he often brought me food or beer if I asked him to. I was running out of money quickly, but I still wasn't so short of money that I needed to worry about saving a couple of dollars on a drug deal.

After Ting hacked the lighter and prepared a boat and a gun for me, he left me to smoke alone. It had been a month since I last smoked alone. I mean, I had the odd secret candy on my own in the bathroom, but apart from that I had always smoked around people. I switched over to one of the music channels on the TV and then put two candies on a boat. I started smoking. I had never put two candies on a boat before. It felt kind of extravagant, but it was nice to have the freedom to do it. If I tried to put two candies on one boat when Fon was around, she would complain the whole time I smoked it, so it wasn't worth the hassle.

I smoked the two candies in a couple of minutes. I felt good. I have heard that cocaine makes you feel like superman, like you can run through walls. In comparison, candy has a very mild affect. Mainly, candy makes you happy – it simply makes you feel good. Candy makes you like people that you would not normally like. But it also makes you very aware and switched on. At no point do you feel 'high' or groggy. It also makes you feel confident and horny, and it gives you an almighty energy boost.

My friend, Keith, was always on the move. He would pop into my apartment for a while, then he would rush off to meet someone at the other side of town, and he could carry on like that, buzzing here and there for three or four days straight, without ever slowing down. I was the complete opposite. I was always worried about my heart, so even though I got a huge energy boost from smoking candy, I usually tried to sit down or lay down so that I could slow my heartbeat down.

I made a new boat and started smoking my third candy. It was nice to smoke on my own, but it was also scary to be alone in my room with drugs. While I was smoking my third candy, I thought I heard some slight movements coming from the hallway a couple of times, so I rushed to the window and peaked through the curtains. The hallway was empty. I sat back down. A few minutes later I suddenly heard a lot of heavy footsteps getting louder and louder as they came down the hall. They stopped near my door and people started talking in Lao. I could hear both male and female voices. I melted the top of the gun quickly, cut it into small pieces, and then I brought the remaining candy and the boat into the bathroom. I worried that maybe someone had seen Ting leave my room and the police had come to catch me. I expected the door to be kicked down at any moment. I held the boat and the candy above the toilet, ready to drop them in and flush them if anybody tried to come into my room. I listened carefully to see if I could recognize my landlord's voice. Perhaps she was showing potential tenants the room across the hallway, or perhaps she was bringing the police to catch me. After a few minutes, the door across the hallway opened and then closed again, and after that I couldn't hear anything. They must have gone inside. I was relieved. As much as she annoyed me at times, I felt much safer smoking with Fon.

After smoking three candies, I sat back on the sofa and messaged Fon. The three candies were having an effect on me. I suddenly missed her. She replied to my message quickly, saying that she was at home with her family and that she hoped I could sleep more. I had a shower and smoked two more candies before I put on clothes. All my clothes smelled terrible, especially my T-shirts. I had not washed my clothes in over two weeks. I didn't have a washing machine in my apartment, so if I wanted to get my clothes cleaned I had to bring them to a guesthouse in falang town and then collect them the next day. But there were loads of reasons why it was hard for me to go outside my apartment and do things. First of all, I hated going out during the day when I smoked candy because candy made me very sensitive to the sun. Secondly, after I smoked, all I wanted to do was lie down in bed and make sure my heart didn't explode. Thirdly, I hated leaving Fon alone in our apartment because I was worried that she would invite a guy over while I was away, and I was also worried that she would not answer the door for me when I came back. She might pretend to be asleep and leave me locked out for hours. For all these reasons, a simple thing like bringing my clothes to be washed was a very difficult task to carry out.

In falang town, tuk-tuk drivers wait for customers outside falang bars or on street corners, but not many falangs came to my neighborhood, so tuk-tuk drivers didn't either. When I left my apartment, I knew that I would have to make the twenty minute walk to Samlo Pub unless I could wave down a passing tuk-tuk on the way. As I was walking along Rue Setthathilath, I kept looking behind me to see if any tuk-tuks were coming. The sweat was pouring off me. I didn't want to walk all the way to the bar. My clothes were already smelly and I didn't want to push my heart too much. Fortunately, a ladyboy I knew named Khek drove passed me on her scooter on the other side of the road. I called out her name and gestured for her to come to my side of the road. She must have thought that I wanted to be her customer.

"I just need a lift to Samlo," I told her when she pulled up alongside me on her scooter.

She looked annoyed.

"Why you call me over just for this?" she asked. "I look for customer now."

We weren't friends. We only knew each other because we had played pool together a few times in Samlo. She was right to be annoyed.

"I'll give you 20,000 kip if you bring me to Samlo," I offered.

"30,000." (3 dollars)

I agreed to pay her price. It was way too much for a three minute ride on the back of her scooter, but it saved me walking for another fifteen minutes.

"Don't drop me off in front of Samlo," I told Khek. "Drop me off at Namphu Fountain and I will walk the rest of the way."

"You don't want people see you with ladyboy, right?"

"No, no, it's not that. It's just..."

"It's okay. I drop you off at Namphu Fountain. No worry."

'Falang town' is a loose term to describe the tourist area by the river in Vientiane. It consists of three main roads and about a dozen side streets. The road along the river is mainly lined with nondescript buildings, and they have bars, restaurants and various stores on the ground floor. There are three really famous bars in falang town: Samlo, Bor Pen Nyang and Khop Chai Deu. Bor Pen Nyang (a rooftop bar) is located on the road by the river. There are about half a dozen side streets linking the road by the river to the next road. There were a couple of nice small hotels on these side streets, and there were some new buildings being built when I was there, but these streets tended to be underdeveloped. There were several rundown guesthouses, cheap restaurants, and a couple of second hand book shops on these side streets. There were even large areas of wasteland between some buildings. It was strange that grass could be let grow on this kind of prime real estate in the middle of the tourist area and only about thirty meters in from the river. Sometimes it was hard to believe that this was really a capital city. It was the most laid-back city I had ever seen, but that's why I liked it.

The other two famous bars, Samlo and Khop Chai Deu, are located on the second road in from the river. The second road is in the middle of falang town, but it is an oddly quiet road because one side of the road is mostly taken up by two old, large temple complexes that have paint peeling off the walls. The walls of these complexes line one side of the main road, meaning most of the businesses on this road are on the other side. Directly across from one of these temple complexes is Samlo bar, and about one hundred meters down the road is Khob Chai Deu and Namphu fountain. There are some nice examples of French Colonial architecture along this road. Some of these colonial buildings have been converted into restaurants and guesthouses. It was cool to see old Lao temples and French colonial buildings side by side. It's one of the charming things about Vientiane. The third road in from the river, however, lacked any charm. There was a luxury hotel and a couple of expensive restaurants and bars, but there was nothing there for me.

I arrived at Samlo at about ten o'clock. Samlo was always quiet at this time. I liked it at this time because I could sit at the bar on my own and enjoy the music while I drank beer. Before eleven o'clock the owner played rock music, like Oasis, Kings of Leon and The Beatles, but as the place started to fill up, he switched to hip hop and dance music. I greeted the owner and the three bartenders as I took my seat at the bar. I got on really well with one of the bartenders, Sit, so we greeted each other warmly.

"Why you no come here long time?" she asked me.

"Sorry. I'll start to come here more, like before."

"You too skinny now. What happened you?" Sit asked me, kind of shocked, kind of teasing me.

"Just exercise and diet. You always said that I was too fat."

"Yes, you were too fat before, but now you too skinny. Not good. I worry you."

"Don't worry about me. I'm okay."

Sit handed me an empty glass and a large bottle of Beer Lao.

"You want ice?" she asked.

"Yes, please."

Lao people drink beer with ice, and so do the falangs who live in Laos.

Sit leaned her arms on the beer taps and spoke with me for a while. Apart from me, there were only two other customers in the bar – an old white guy and a young Lao woman. I overheard the old guy talking and gathered that he was an English teacher in Thailand and that he was only here on a visa run. He was due to collect his new visa at the Thai Embassy in a few days and then catch a bus straight back to Bangkok.

Before I met Fon, I used to come to Samlo nearly every night for about seven months. I knew all the regular customers and their habits. For example, I knew that between ten and eleven o'clock a beautiful Lao woman named Noy would arrive and sit on her own at the bar. As expected, Noy came to Samlo ten minutes after me, and as soon as she sat down she ordered a glass of red wine, just like she always did. In Laos, a lot of ladyboys choose the name Noy because in Lao it means 'small', but this Noy was definitely a woman. She always wore an elegant, slim-fitting dress. Noy was sexy, and a lot of men liked her, but she didn't go with many men. She had a sponsor in Europe who sent her money every month, and he visited Laos a couple of times a year. I'm sure she did sleep around a bit, but she was discrete about it because she didn't want

56

her sponsor to hear any rumors about her when he came to Laos. A lot of the girls who hung around falang town had sponsors. I often saw these girls walking along the street with their sponsors. Some of them would say hello to me proudly and introduce me to their 'boyfriend'. But others would pretend not to know me, and of course I would pretend not to know them because the simple fact that she knows me means that she comes to falang town. Why does she come to falang town? She doesn't work in a hotel, a restaurant, an internet café, or a bar, so why does she come? She comes to falang town to drink in a falang bar. Falang bars are more expensive than other bars in Laos, so why does she go to a falang bar? To meet falangs. Why? For sex. For money. Any falang who has lived in Laos can see this situation very clearly, but a falang who visits Laos for the first time can easily be fooled. A falang meets a beautiful woman in Samlo. The woman says that she works in a hair salon. She says that she likes to come to this bar to dance and play pool with her friends, and perhaps practice English too. But this is all bullshit. It's all a game. These women all have a plan. If they just want to get money quickly and move on, they will offer the falang sex for 250,000 kip. Of course the falang can haggle and bring the price down. But, if the girl plays it right, she can make the foreigner believe that she is a good girl who is worth holding onto. In this case, the girl won't ask for money upfront. She will find out early how long the foreigner plans to stay in Laos. He might only stay in Laos for a few days, in which case the girl will try to stay with him for those few days and she will be as nice as possible to him the whole time, and perhaps she will even bring him to her family home to make him feel more emotionally attached to her life. She will gradually let him know about how poor her family is and how she needs money for this and that. These girls have so many tricks. At the end of the two days, the falang will inevitably give her money out of the kindness of his heart, or perhaps he will give some money to pay for some emergency situation that her family is going through. The falang will return to his home country but he will stay in contact with the girl. After about a month, the girl will mention that she has a problem and that she needs him to send her money. If he refuses, she will say that she has no other choice but to start working in a bar as a prostitute. She will say that she really doesn't want to do it, but it is the only way she can earn the money she needs quickly enough. If the falang sends the money, the same situation might occur a month later. If the girl is not too pushy, the falang might become her sponsor. But, of course, the falang doesn't know that he is a sponsor. He is under the illusion that he is her boyfriend.

One night Fon and I smoked with her friend, Tuey, and a fellow falang in our room. Tuey and the falang had hooked up the night before in Samlo. It was about three AM in the morning when Tuey's phone started to ring.

"Put TV on mute," Tuey ordered me.

Tuey put her index finger to her mouth to signal to me and the other falang to be quiet.

"What's going on?" I whispered to Fon.

"It's her boyfriend in Germany."

We all remained completely silent while Tuey spoke with her

sponsor.

"I in home, honey. I sleepy now, so I no talk long."

While Tuey talked with the German guy, her voice sounded lovely, but she looked really bored. She held the phone to her ear with her left shoulder, and she used her two free hands to make a boat. I wanted to smoke candy, but I knew that the bubbling water in the gun would be too noisy. If I tried to go into the bathroom, the German guy might hear me open and close the door. I didn't want to make a problem for Tuey. I could see that Tuey wanted to finish the call after a couple of minutes, but the German guy kept asking about her family and friends. After about ten minutes, Tuey was rolling her eyes a lot and she looked annoyed, but her voice remained soft and lovely. As soon as Tuey finished the call, she ordered me to turn up the volume on the TV and she started smoking candy again. Tuey went back to the falang's hotel room before sunrise. When they left, Fon told me the good news.

"Tuey say she buy us candy tomorrow. She come here tomorrow at two PM."

"Why?"

"Tuey say the falang leave Laos tomorrow, so he give her money. And German man send her Western Union tomorrow. Tuey have many money tomorrow so she want treat us. She say we buy her candy many times so she want to buy for us."

Apart from Noy, there were many other Lao people and falangs who could be seen in Samlo nearly every night. Cat was another of those who always came to Samlo before eleven o' clock. Cat was a tall, slim, quite masculine ladyboy. She didn't have fake breasts and it looked like any hormones that she might have taken didn't have much of an effect on her. Cat and Fon were the only two Lao people I knew who owed a car. Everybody else used a scooter. Fon's ex-fiance from England bought the car for her, but as far as I know Cat bought her car herself. It was a long, black car that must have been about fifteen years old. It was a bit of a banger, but it did the job, and I'm sure it was still much more expensive than the heap-of-shit scooters that most of the women drove around on. Cat owned a small hair salon in Vientiane, a couple of kilometers outside of falang town, and she was saving money to open up her own bar in falang town. All the other ladyboys who came to Samlo were just looking to find a falang who would take them for short time, but Cat was different. To me, it seemed like she just wanted to socialize with people and have a good time. Perhaps she was looking for a boyfriend but she definitely wasn't offering herself to falangs for money.

Before eleven o'clock, I put my name on the list for a game of pool. The bar had already filled up a little bit so there were a couple of names ahead of me on the list. At eleven o' clock the owner, who also acted as the DJ, changed the music from rock to dance music. I ordered my third beer from Sit.

"You don't look happy. What wrong?" Sit asked, as she took my money.

"I'm happy. I just don't like this music."

In truth, I felt a bit bored. I wanted to smoke candy again. Every time the door swung open I turned around to see if it was Keith. I also remembered that Ted said that he would come to Samlo that night, but Ted wasn't good at sticking to plans. He always got distracted by women or drugs, and he also had to prepare for his trip to Thailand. I took out my phone to text Keith, but I was surprised to see that I had half a dozen missed calls and as many messages from him. He said that he wanted to smoke and that he would pick me up outside Samlo at 11:30. It worked out perfectly. I could play pool and finish my beer.

Suddenly a lot of falangs who lived in Laos came into the bar. I realized that it must be a Friday or a Saturday (I often lost track of the days), because that's when those falangs came out in numbers. There were several falangs (mostly males but a couple of females) in their twenties who worked as English teachers in Vientiane. They seemed to go out drinking in falang bars almost every night. They didn't need any qualifications or university degree to get a job as an English teacher, so they were able to get a job and a work visa easily. I heard they earned about seven or eight hundred dollars a month, which allowed them to have a really fun life in Laos. But apart from these young English teachers, most of the falangs who lived in Laos were middle aged, and their jobs varied a lot. They tended to only come to falang bars at the weekend. A lot of these middle aged falangs were bar owners or restaurant owners. There was also an accountant, a financial advisor, an old guy who helped to detect mines, and a consultant who was working on one of the large dams along one of the Mekong river's estuaries. There seemed to be a lot of foreign consultants working in and around Vientiane. I guess this is because Laos lacked expertise in certain fields.

Several falangs I knew tapped me on the shoulder and greeted me when they came into Samlo. One of them was a guy called Paul. He was the only English teacher I knew who was old enough to be my dad. Paul taught English in a couple of schools in Vientiane. He had broken his right leg in a scooter accident a month previous and he was still wearing a cast. A Lao man had come speeding down a dark alley without any lights and he crashed into Paul at a terrible speed. Paul was lucky that he only broke his leg, and the Lao guy was even luckier because he escaped completely unscathed. Paul sued the guy, but he couldn't pay Paul anything so he was sent to prison. I once asked Paul if he ever considered dropping the charge so that the Lao guy could come out of prison, but Paul said that he deserved to be in prison for at least as long as he wore the cast.

Another falang to come greet me was another English guy in his fifties named Brian. He owned a bar next to Lao Plaza. He closed the bar at eleven o'clock every night and then came to Samlo for a few beers. In his bar, Brian had heard a lot of cautionary tales about Lao women from his customers and he sometimes shared them with me. Perhaps all these cautionary tales are the reason why he didn't have a Lao girlfriend. He only seemed to be interested in running his bar, having a few drinks at night and playing pool. One time he told me that him and his other falang friends sometimes crossed the Thai border and had a Guinness party in Nong Khai - the nearest Thai city. There wasn't any draught Guinness in Laos, so they had to travel to another country for it.

While I was sitting at the bar waiting for my turn to play pool, one of the workers came to me and said, "Your friend want you go talk with him."

She pointed at one of the three booths against the back wall. An Irish guy I knew called Danny was sitting in one of the booths with his younger Lao girlfriend. Out of politeness I went over and sat with him. Danny had a thick Dublin accent. I never asked him his age, but he once told me that his two sons were around my age. He was very stocky, he had a skin head and both his arms were covered in tattoos. One of his front upper teeth was chipped, and he had a habit of running his tongue along the chipped part when he was bored or lost in thought. Danny looked like a tough guy, but he was really kind and friendly. The problem was that Danny was a bit of a Billy bullshitter. It was exhausting listening to him sometimes. He had lived in Laos far longer than me so his opinions about the country trumped mine every time. For example, one time he told me that the Lao government keeps records on all the falangs who live in Laos.

"I don't know about that," I told him, not believing him for a second.

"They do. I'm tellin' ya," he said, with unmoving conviction. "They have spies all around falang town. They know who you are staying with, who you are meeting, where you drink at night, and it's all kept in a file they have on you."

"I don't think the police have the resources for that," I told him. "The police don't even work at night over here."

"It's all done through spies. You know it's a communist country,

63

right?"

"Yeah, I know, but..."

"Trust me. They are watching. Make no mistake about it."

There was no point arguing with him. Sometimes, however, he did make sense. The first time I got talking with Danny in Samlo he told me something interesting about traffic lights in Laos.

"Laos is a really backward country," he said. "Only about ten years ago they introduced traffic lights into Vientiane. But a lot of people didn't know what the traffic lights were for, so they caused a lot of accidents. Some cars and motorbikes would suddenly stop at the red light, and the car behind would just keep going and crash into the back of them. It was mayhem."

When Danny first told me this story, I completely dismissed it. I thought he was just having a rant about Lao people. The next day I went to Talat Sao (the morning market) to buy some DVDs. There is an old outdoor section and a new indoor section in Talat Sao. The DVD store I wanted to go to was on the second floor of the new indoor section. On the first floor I saw two Lao women in their forties standing at the bottom of the escalator. They didn't know how to step onto the escalator. They couldn't figure out the timing. I bought some DVDs and when I came back down the escalator, the two women were gone. They had either figured out the timing or they had given up and gone outside to the old section. Laos was a very underdeveloped country. Seeing those two women struggling to step onto the escalator made me think that Danny might have been right about the traffic lights causing mayhem on the streets of Vientiane.

I only sat with Danny and his girlfriend for a few minutes. I asked him what he had been up to recently and he said he was looking for a place to open a new bar. He used to own a bar about ten minutes outside falang town, but it closed down after a year. He said that his girlfriend knew someone who could get me a work visa for a year if I was interested, but I told him about my plans to go home in August. Before he could reply, Sit came over and told me it was my turn to play pool. I brought my beer to the pool table and I was a little disappointed to see that my opponent was a tall, young Chinese guy called Ting. In Samlo it was winner stays on, so I wasn't happy to be playing Ting. He was easily the best pool player in falang town. If you won six games in a row in Samlo you got a free beer. Ting could go twenty games in a row without losing, so usually he didn't accept the free beer. He knew that if he accepted it every time, things might become a little awkward between him and the owner. I took one shot and then Ting cleared the table. I shook his hand and went back to the bar.

My seat had been taken. It's awkward to stay in a bar on your own if you don't have a seat. I walked around the bar briefly. I only knew a handful of the falangs in the bar, but I knew dozens of the Lao people. Out of the Lao people, only a couple of them were men, and they were gay. There were also a couple of ladyboys there too, but usually, except for Cat, the ladyboys were not regular customers because they didn't have the money to buy an expensive drink in a falang bar every night. Samlo was starting to fill up and I knew that there would be a sudden influx of people after twelve o'clock. Twelve o' clock was an important time for Samlo because that was when the other two main falang bars (Khop Chai Deu and Bor Pen Nyang) closed. Samlo stayed open until two o'clock. Lao women and falangs usually went to the other falang bars first and then came to Samlo at the end of the night.

I placed my beer on the bar and went to the bathroom. There was a queue. There was a ladyboy in front of me in the queue – the toilets were unisex. I recognized the ladyboy. She came to Samlo sometimes. When she realized that there was a falang behind her, she turned around and greeted me.

"Hi, I'm Noy," she said.

This Noy was very young and feminine. She didn't have breasts, but her body was very petite.

"I see you in Vang Vieng," Noy said to me.

I had heard this from different ladyboys several times before. It is a conversation starter that a lot of ladyboys in Vientiane like to use. The ladyboy says that they saw the falang in Vang Vieng because they know that nearly every falang who comes to Laos ends up visiting Vang Vieng. Most tourists who come to Vientiane come from Vang Vieng, so the ladyboy knows that if she says, 'I saw you in Vang Vieng,' there is a good chance that the falang will think that the ladyboy had actually seen him in Vang Vieng a few days previous. He might think that this is an amazing coincidence and it might make him more open to talking with the ladyboy. And from there anything can happen. But I had been through this very same conversation with several ladyboys before, so I just told

Noy straight, that I had not been to Vang Vieng in months and that I lived in Vientiane. She didn't seem happy with my answer. She muttered something under her breath and turned her back to me.

When I came out from the bathroom, my glass of beer had disappeared. I guess Sit had cleared it away by mistake. It was already 11:25, so I decided to wait outside for Keith. There were a couple of cars parked outside Samlo, but the side of the road and the footpath were full of scooters. While I was waiting outside, a Lao woman I knew named Apple stopped and talked with me. I remembered Keith had once told me that he had been in a relationship with Apple.

"Walt, I no see you in long time. Where you been?" Apple asked me.

"Nowhere, just around."

"Where is Fon? She inside?"

"No, she's at home with her family."

"So come inside and we can drink together."

"I can't. I'm waiting for Keith. He came back to Laos today."

"English Keith?" she looked surprised and a bit repulsed.

"Yeah, English Keith. He is coming here now. You want to say hello to him?"

"No, thanks. I go inside. You should be careful him," Apple warned me. "You good man, Walt. You kind. Be careful him."

While I was waiting for Keith outside Samlo, I saw a lot of beautiful Lao women arrive on their motorbikes. I also saw a man holding a machine gun across the street. These armed guards patrolled the streets at night instead of the police. I had seen these armed guards dozens of times but it never made me feel afraid. In fact, I always felt incredibly safe in Vientiane.

Instead of waiting outside Samlo, I messaged Keith to tell him to meet me in front of Namphu fountain. I fancied a short walk. On my way there I heard a voice saying, "Blowjob, free."

I looked to my left and saw a tall ladyboy standing in a dark side street. I didn't recognize her.

"I know you smoke. Me too," she said. "I have room end of this street."

I kept walking. I could hear music coming from Khop Chai Deu. They had live music most nights. I couldn't see the musicians when I walked passed, but I could tell that they were two Lao guys with a guitar and a keyboard. They were playing *In My Life* by The Beatles. It sounded good, but the pronunciation was a bit off. When I arrived at Namphu fountain I had still not received a message from Keith. I sat on one of the many benches around the fountain and listened to the music from Khop Chai Deu. This was a particularly nice part of falang town, with some expensive looking French restaurants and new Western style bakeries and cafes. I gave Keith a call but he didn't answer. Then I saw a woman called Mem sit down on one of the benches at the other side of the fountain. She was one of the last people I wanted to bump into. She was a nightmare! During my first month in Laos I bought a phone and I sat down near the fountain to set it up and put in credit. Mem was sitting nearby, and when she saw that I was having difficulty putting in the credit, she came over and helped me. Her English was amazing and she had a very strong American accent. I'm not sure if it's true, but she said she moved to America with her family when she was young and she had only recently returned to Laos to take care of her grandmother. Mem was average height for a Lao woman, but she was very wide and stocky. She wore baggy jeans and a red polo shirt. She had short hair and a weird looking elongated face with a very strong jaw. The shape and proportions of her face and mouth looked wrong. Her mouth was also crooked. I thought she was a lesbian, but then she mentioned that she had a German boyfriend. Mem seemed normal at first, but the more we talked the stranger the conversation became. She had a filthy mouth. She started telling me about a feud between her uncle and her father, and while she was telling the story she kept calling her uncles, aunts and cousins 'motherfuckers', 'cunts' and 'stupid bitches'. She also kept saying things like 'Lao people are not like you and me', and then she would go on to say how Lao people are not educated and don't have any manners. As soon as there was a natural lull in the conversation, I told her I had to go meet someone. That evening, when I was in my room getting ready to go out for dinner, I heard a knock on my door. When I opened the door, I was shocked to see Mem standing there with her female friend. I instantly realized that when we talked by the fountain I had told her what guesthouse I was staying in.

"This my friend. Let's go for dinner together, dude," she said, in what now sounded like an exaggerated American accent.

Her friend was beautiful, but I didn't want to be around Mem.

"I have a plan to meet my friend," I said.

For the next five evenings Mem came knocking on my door with her friend to ask me to join them for dinner and drinks. She also came looking for me in Samlo a couple of times. While I was playing pool, Mem explained that her friend doesn't speak English but she would make a really good girlfriend. She kept repeating the same shit over and over again. 'She very good girl. Not same other fucking bitches in this bar', 'She never had a falang boyfriend before', and 'She will make you very happy if you take care of her'.

Eventually she gave up. She stopped coming to my room and whenever she saw me in Samlo she greeted me but she never stopped to talk to me. That suited me just fine. For a long time I couldn't figure out why she had tried to push her friend on me, but then one of the girls in Samlo told me that Mem is a lesbian and her 'friend' is actually her girlfriend. Her friend didn't speak a word of English, so Mem helped her find falang customers or boyfriends and they probably split the money.

Now here she was again sitting in almost exactly the same place next to the fountain, probably looking for another falang to cling on to. Keith finally messaged me. He had a problem with his bike and he was getting it fixed near Bor Pen Nyang bar by the river. It was only five minutes away, so I told him I would walk to him. I crossed the road at Khop Chai Deu and passed the corner where ladyboys gather every night. I don't know why they gathered at that particular corner. There weren't many guesthouses or hotels around that area, so if a falang did want to bring one of them back to his room, he would have to walk quite a long way with a ladyboy on his arm. Perhaps ladyboys liked that corner because it was directly across from Khob Chai Deu, which was a popular bar among older falang.

There were five ladyboys at the corner when I passed. I didn't recognize any of them so I kept my head down and walked by.

"I know you candy boy," one of them said, but I didn't acknowledge their comment.

I didn't know any of these ladyboys, yet one of them knew that I smoked candy. Perhaps I smoked with one of her friends before or maybe she was Ting's friend. Maybe somebody in Samlo or Don Chan pointed me out to her and told her I liked candy. Falang town was a small place. Or maybe she just knew I used candy by how skinny and pale I looked. I walked down one of the dark side streets towards the river. A couple of the bars and restaurants facing the river were still open, but there weren't many people around. Across the river I could see lights coming from a couple of houses in rural Thailand. I remembered that Ted would be making his way across that river in a couple of hours to see his daughter for the first time.

As I was walking along the road, I watched people pass by on their scooters. They were mostly young Lao men and women. I made eye contact with a woman who was driving on the far side of the road. She did a quick U-turn and slowed down alongside me.

"Where you go mister?" she asked.

This Lao woman looked a little older than me. She was a little chubby but sexy.

"I'm going to meet my friend," I replied.

"Where you stay?"

"Back that way," I said, pointing behind me, trying to be as vague as I could.

We had never seen each other before, so she didn't know that I lived in Laos.

"You stay alone?" she asked.

"Yes, kind of."

"I go your room now, okay?"

"No, sorry. I have to meet my friend."

"No problem," she said with a smile, and then she drove off out of sight.

A lot of women and ladyboys drove up and down the roads in falang town looking for customers. To be honest, before I met Fon, I often met women this way. It was so easy. You make eye contact when the woman drives passed. She does a U-turn. You jump on the back of her scooter and you are back in your room within a couple of minutes. It was very discreet. I was living in Laos so discretion was important to me. I didn't want to be seen leaving Samlo with a lot of different woman.

As I approached Bor Pen Nyang I passed a group of five tuk-tuk drivers who were waiting at the corner for customers.

"Yaba," one of them whispered.

It wasn't even a question. He just whispered it to let me know it was available.

"Marijauna," another one of them whispered. "Girl. Massage.

Where you go? What you want?"

"No thanks," I nodded politely.

Tuk-tuk drivers gave me the creeps. I'm not sure why, but I didn't trust them.

When I passed Bor Pen Nyang, there were a lot of motorbikes outside but it was almost midnight so people were starting to leave. I couldn't see Keith anywhere. I pulled out my phone to give him a call but just at that moment he pulled up alongside me on his scooter. I jumped on his bike and we drove off. He did a quick U-turn and drove back the way I had come from. Keith reached his hand back to shake my hand

"What's up man?" he said very warmly. "I missed you."

Keith was a very friendly and outgoing person, so it was easy to befriend him. We were about the same age, we both had a really strong candy habit, we both liked to drink beer and go to falang bars, and neither of us worked so we could just hangout and smoke all day and night.

"It's good to have you back," I told Keith. "How have you been?"

"I'm alright. Same shit," he said. "I'll tell you about it when we get to your place. You have candy?"

"Yeah. I have five."

"We'll need more. Do you know anyone we can call?"

"Yeah, I can call Ting."

"The gay lad?"

"Yeah, that's him. I'll call him when we get to my place."

Keith had been staying with his parents in England for the past three weeks, resting and eating well, but he didn't look much different for it. Keith was a naturally skinny guy, so he didn't tend to lose much weight when he smoked candy. The only difference I noticed in him was his clothes and his haircut. The last time I saw Keith, his brownish blonde hair had grown out over his ears and down his forehead, and he wore flip flops, baggy shorts and tank tops every day. But now, on his first day back in Laos, he looked much cleaner and more respectable. His hair was short and he was wearing sneakers, jeans and a blue short-sleeved shirt. Keith, however, noticed a big difference in me.

When we arrived at my place, he took a good look at me and said, "You look like shit."

"Compared to when you saw me last?"

"Yeah. You look much worse. You look skinnier and paler."

"But I was smoking a lot when I saw you last. I was skinny as fuck then too."

"But you didn't look this bad."

I took the five candies from under the bed and threw them to Keith.

"Can we share these?" he asked. "I'll pay you back when Ting comes. "

"Yeah, you take three. Two is enough for me at the moment."

Keith placed one of the candies in his mouth and washed it down with some water.

"Why did you do that?" I asked. "Isn't it dangerous?"

"I don't think so. I heard it's safer."

74

"But why bother doing it? Isn't smoking the best way to take it?"

"Some people swallow it. Sometimes when I'm in a bar or a club, I just go to the toilet and swallow one to give myself a boost."

I had never seen anybody swallow one of these pink pills before. It seemed dangerous and kind of disgusting. Keith was a bit agitated when I told him that Ting couldn't come. He was way outside Vientiane. Keith's dealer was also unavailable.

"We have enough," I said. "Let's smoke two each and then go to Don Chan."

"I was hoping to do a few more," Keith said. "I arrived in Lao this morning but I've only had five candies all day."

"Let's finish these quickly and if we have time maybe we can go buy some off a tuk-tuk driver before we go to Don Chan," I suggested.

Keith looked around my room, and when he saw some make-up and girl's clothes, he asked, "Who are you staying with?"

"Fon."

"You're still with her?" he asked, surprised.

"Yeah, she is with her family tonight. I saw Apple outside Samlo, just before you came."

"The Apple with big tits and short hair?" Keith asked.

"Yes, that Apple."

"I was with her before, you know?"

"Yeah, you told me. How did you guys hook up?"

"I was staying in Vang Vieng at the time. I was actually working in one of the bars there. They let me DJ sometimes. Apple was in Vang

Vieng with one of her mates, so we hooked up and she stayed with me for a few months. But then she had to go to Thailand to meet her Australian sponsor. He came over for a holiday."

"I didn't know you used to stay in Vang Vieng."

Even before I had become friends with Keith, I had seen him whizzing around the streets of Vientiane on his scooter every day. To me, he was like the mascot of falang town.

"I used to love Vang Vieng, man. Party all day by the river, half naked falang and Lao women everywhere. Drugs everywhere. Cheap guesthouses. Actually, Vang Vieng is the reason I decided to stay in Laos. I came travelling in Southeast Asia about five years ago with a bunch of my mates. When we came to Vang Vieng, I liked it so much that I ended up staying there for the rest of the year. I missed my flight back to England and everything."

"But isn't candy expensive there? I heard it's about 50,000 kip for one, and sometimes even 100,000."

"Yeah, it's expensive, but if you get to know the right people you can get it for about 35,000 kip. But that's only if you stay there for a long time and if you make the right friends. You can buy it in most of the bars there, so you can smoke it in the bar's bathroom, no problem. They provide the boat, the gun and the lighter. Everything is pre-prepared."

"I might go to Vang Vieng for a while next week. My rent is almost up on this place so I might pack up my stuff and fuck off to Vang Vieng for a while on my own."

"Without Fon?"

"Yeah, without Fon. I need to get away from candy for a while. If I'm alone in Vang Vieng, I'm sure I won't smoke. My flight back home is in about six weeks. Maybe I can stay in Vang Vieng for two weeks and relax, and then come back to Vientiane for the last month."

"It sounds like a good idea. It will be shitty not to have you in Vientiane, but it looks like you need a break."

Keith made the ugliest boat I had ever seen. Before he put the candy on it, I offered to make him a better boat, but he said that he just wanted to smoke quickly. From his pocket he pulled out a tiny mouthwash bottle with a hole in it. He used it as a gun.

"I never thought to use a mouthwash bottle as a gun," I told him. "Good idea."

"Yeah, it's handy. I can carry it around in my pocket."

Keith placed both of his candies on his boat and he used a normal sized flame when he smoked. When you are smoking candy, even after you turn off the flame the candy continues to melt and produce smoke for about another five seconds. So, most people turn off the flame about five seconds before they stop inhaling. Keith was the only person I had ever seen who pulled the gun out of his mouth as soon as he turned off the flame. A thick string of smoke rose up between us.

"What a waste of candy!" I said.

"Fuck it!" Keith said. "We will buy more anyway."

Keith jumped to his feet and started walking around the room. He always looked agitated and restless. He checked his phone and fixed his hair in the mirror.

I tried his mini gun. The good thing was that it was very quiet because the bottle couldn't hold much water, but it wasn't comfortable to use because the size of the bottle meant that I could only inhale very slowly. I didn't know this at first, so I burnt the candy quickly and I wasn't able to suck in all the smoke quickly enough. Keith saw the smoke rising up towards the ceiling and he commented, "You are wasting more than me."

I had another go off the gun, only this time I burnt the candy very slowly. Keith and I took it in turns to use the gun, but near the end Keith didn't want to wait for his turn so he rolled up a one thousand kip note and smoked it directly from the boat. This meant that the smoke didn't get filtered through any water.

"What's it like when you smoke it without the gun?" I asked.

"It tastes like shit," he said, sticking his tongue in and out of his mouth to get rid of the horrible taste.

When Keith had finished his candy, I still had one left. I asked him to tell me about his time back home while I smoked.

"There's absolutely fuck all to tell, to be honest," he said. "I thought I'd work for at least three or four months and gather a good bit of money, but I decided to sell my car instead and come back. I still owe my parents money from the last trip. They fuckin' hate the idea of me coming over here. They don't get it all. They never say it to me directly, but they must know that I'm up to no good over here. And I completely screwed them over the last couple of times. You know, I missed my flight the last two times, so my parents had to get me a ticket home, and I've borrowed a ton of money off of them as well. I promised them that this would be my last time coming to Laos. I think they'll disown me if I come back again."

"I'm sure they won't disown you, but they probably think it's a waste of time saving up money in England and then blowing it all in Laos over a few months, and then going back home to repeat the process."

"What do your parents think about you being over here?"

"They don't get it at all," I said. "They think I'm just wasting my time over here. But I haven't asked them to lend me money yet, so they just let me get on with things."

"Do they know you are doing drugs? I mean, do they suspect anything?"

"Probably. They've never asked me directly, but they were shocked by how skinny I was when I went home last time. They must know that I'm up to something over here."

"Same with my parents, but I get so fucking depressed when I go back home. You know, I don't even want to go out and meet up with my friends. It's so much fun over here compared to back home. What's been happening since I've been away?"

"Absolutely nothing," I told Keith. "I've barely been outside the door. Fon and I go to Don Chan most nights at about 2 o'clock. We have one beer, and then we come straight back here."

Keith and Fon had known each other long before they met me. Keith's best friend used to be a guy named Dan, and Dan used to be with Fon's best friend, Neung. I asked Fon several times whether she had ever fucked Keith, but she simply said that she doesn't go with 'crazy falang'. I didn't believe her. They used to smoke candy together a lot, and they were both single, so I was convinced that they had hooked up at some point. I never asked Keith directly because I figured that he would deny it and I thought it would make me look insecure. But as I smoked my last candy, I asked him, "You knew Fon long before me, right? Did she go with a lot of falang?"

"No, I don't think so. She used to hang around Don Chan a lot, but from what I remember she had a sponsor in France, so she didn't really go with falang. I don't remember much about her from that time to be honest, but I remember one night Neung told me and Dan that she thought Fon was amazing at handling falang."

"What did she mean by that?"

"I don't know. She didn't elaborate."

"But you never saw her go with a falang?"

"No, I don't think so."

Sometimes in Samlo a falang tourist would ask me about their new Lao girlfriend. I would say that she is a really nice girl and that she doesn't usually go with falang, even if I had seen her go with a guy for short time the night before. I didn't want to destroy the illusion for the falang or expose the Lao woman. I just wanted to stay out of it. I knew that Keith was covering for Fon, but I didn't hold it against him.

Keith scrunched up his boat and threw it on the floor. This guy was not careful about anything. Whenever he came to my room, he would leave his rubbish on the ground and then leave without a care in the world. I used to be foolish enough to clean up after him, but after a while I just told him straight, "Don't leave guns and boats on the floor like that. Flush the boat down the toilet and take the gun with you."

"Can't I leave the gun here?" Keith asked. "We'll probably come back here later anyway. I'll hide it behind the wardrobe or under the bed."

"I don't like leaving that stuff in my room when I go out. It only takes a minute to make a new gun, so why risk it? If you want to keep that mini gun, you'll have to take it with you. Otherwise, melt the bottle so that nobody can see the hole, and then throw it in the trash."

One thing I found a little suspicious about Keith was that he always seemed to smoke in other people's rooms. In all the time I knew him, I only ever smoked in his room once. Fon always pointed this out.

"Why he no ask you go smoke in his room?" she often asked me.

"Because his room is too far away," I said.

"He have bike. He can bring you. I have car. I can bring you. No problem."

"It's easier this way."

"You really stupid, you know that?" she would say, laughing at me. "He come your room, make a mess and then go. But his room very clean, I'm sure. If police come this room when Keith here, he say it not his room and they let him go. It your room so you in trouble."

Fon had a point. If my room was ever raided, I would be the one in deep trouble because it was my room. The other thing Fon often said about Keith was that he could speak Lao very well. Keith told me he couldn't speak Lao. I saw him try to speak a couple of sentences in Lao before but I could see that he was a complete novice.

"He lie you," Fon told me. "He speak Lao very well but he no show people. He stay in Lao much longer than you. Of course he speak Lao."

I couldn't agree with Fon on this one. I just couldn't imagine any reason why Keith would pretend not to be good at Lao. It seemed more likely that Fon was trying to turn me against him. When I first befriended Keith, Fon wasn't happy about it. She told me that the police followed him sometimes and that he couldn't be trusted. I didn't believe her. I figured that she just didn't want me to have any friends, or perhaps she just didn't want me to be friends with Keith because she was afraid he would tell me something about her.

We flushed the boats down the toilet and Keith put the gun into his pocket. I sat on the sofa and brushed my teeth. While he was waiting, Keith flicked through the channels on the TV. I knew what he was looking for. He turned on one of the Lao TV channels. An immaculately groomed young Lao man was interviewing an old Lao farmer at the side of a rice field.

"She's not on at the moment," Keith said.

I went into the bathroom and spat out the tooth paste.

"Who is not on?" I asked from the bathroom, already knowing what he would say.

"My ex," he said. "Did I ever tell you that I used to go out with a Lao TV presenter?"

"Yeah, about ten fuckin' times. Let's go."

As we drove away from my apartment complex, Keith asked me, "Where are we going? To find a tuk-tuk driver?"

I checked the time. It was only 12:40. There was no point going to Don Chan before two o'clock because it would be empty. Keith often bought candy from tuk-tuk drivers, but I didn't trust them.

"I'd rather not deal with Tuk-tuk drivers," I said.

Keith pulled the scooter over to the side of the road.

"I don't really want to buy from a Tuk-tuk driver either, but it's our only option."

Tuk-tuk drivers waited on street corners and outside falang bars in falang town. They sold marijuana and candy at an inflated price to falangs.

"How much is candy from a Tuk-tuk driver?" I asked Keith.

"If I find a tuk-tuk driver that I know, maybe I can get them for 30,000, otherwise we'll probably have to pay 35,000 or 40,000. I usually only buy one or two from them at a time when I'm out and about, but we'll probably buy about six, right? Maybe I can get ten for 300,000 thousand."

"No, fuck that!" I said. "I don't want to buy ten from a tuk-tuk driver at the side of the road."

I had another idea. About four hundred meters up from my apartment complex there was a large, old run-down guesthouse. This place was dodgy. Ting practically lived there because he was always there delivering candy to his customers. Falangs did not go to this place unless a girl or a ladyboy brought them there to smoke. It is at the end of a long, dark alley. It's very hard to find. Lao girls and ladyboys like this guesthouse because it is hidden away from the main street and it is cheap. On any one night, there would be a candy party taking place in at least half a dozen of the rooms. This was the guesthouse that I usually went to when I hooked up with women behind Fon's back. I paid 50,000 kip (five dollars) for a room. That was the price for a falang. I guess Lao people paid even less. I told Keith about this guesthouse. He already knew about it - of course he did. He knew every candy spot in the city. Between the two of us, Keith and I knew roughly a hundred candy users, so I reckoned that if we went to the guesthouse and walked the halls for a few minutes, there was a good chance that we would be spotted by someone we knew. Keith agreed to go along with my plan, because even if it failed we would still have enough time to go to falang town and buy candy from a tuk-tuk driver.

4

When we pulled up outside the guesthouse, I realized that it wasn't a good time to come looking for people. Women and ladyboys who came to this type of guesthouse usually smoked candy in their room and then went out to a club at about ten or eleven o'clock, and then they came back to the room after Don Chan at about three or four o'clock and started smoking again. Keith and I arrived at the guesthouse before one AM. We went up to the second floor and walked up and down the hall slowly. All the rooms seemed empty, except for one. In this room the volume on the TV was turned up quite high, and the people inside were speaking very quietly. This was a sure sign that they were smoking candy inside. We walked past the room a few times and we started coughing loudly on purpose so that somebody would peep out the window at us. We saw somebody peep through the curtains, but after that there wasn't any reaction.

"I guess they don't know us," I said. "Let's try the third floor."

All the rooms on the third floor seemed empty. If somebody was smoking candy inside one of the rooms, we would have been able to hear the TV or some music playing inside to cover the sound of bubbling water from a gun. But there was only silence on the third floor. When we went down to the first floor, we noticed that the lights were on in the room at the end of the hall. At first, we only heard a group of Lao people chatting, but then we suddenly heard the sound of bubbling water. The people inside were smoking and they weren't even trying to hide the sound. Keith and I were confident that we would know at least one person in that room, but neither of us knew what to do next. Without giving it any thought, Keith knocked on the door. We could hear the people in the room start whispering.

"Why did you do that?" I asked Keith. "What are we going to say to them?"

"They will let us in when they see that we are falang," Keith said confidently.

We could see the curtains being pulled slightly to one side and I thought I could see two eyes peering out at us. But then the curtains closed again and we were left standing in the hallway. Keith knocked on the door again.

"Who you?" a man inside the room asked.

"We are Noy's friends," I said.

Given that 'Noy' is such a common name, I figured there was a good chance that there would be a person named Noy in the room, or at least they would have a close friend named Noy.

"What you want?" the man asked us.

"We want to smoke candy...chocolate," Keith said.

I wish that he had not said it so loudly. I thought we should be a bit more secretive about this type of thing, but Keith wasn't a cautious person.

We could hear the group whispering together. After a brief discussion, the door opened slowly and a chubby young Lao man opened the door and welcomed us inside.

I had been in that very same room a month earlier with a girl that I had met in Don Chan, so I knew that there was a bathroom to the right as you enter the room, and I knew that there would be a double bed on the right after we passed the bathroom. There were two skinny, middle aged men sitting together on the bed. They were constantly touching each other, so it was easy to see that they were a couple. I quickly realized that the guy who had let us in was also gay. He was very feminine. A young Lao woman was sitting on the floor next to the bed. She stood up and brought us two wooden chairs from the corner of the room. Except for the two chairs and the bed, the room was completely bare.

All of them spoke a little bit of English, but the young guy who had welcomed us into the room was the best speaker. His name was Kun. He asked us again what we wanted.

"We want to smoke," I said awkwardly.

I felt foolish and vulnerable as I muttered this sentence. I scanned the room quickly. I had heard the sound of bubbling water when I stood outside the room, but now that I was inside I couldn't see any gun or boats.

"So why you come here?" Kun asked us.

"Our friend, Noy, stayed in this room before," I lied. "We thought she was still here so we came to meet her. We wanted to buy candy from her."

Kun spoke with one of the guys on the bed in Lao.

"How many candy you buy?" Kun asked us. "My friend sell five for 100,000 kip."

"Fuck, that's cheap!" I said to Keith. "Let's just get ten and give them one each."

Keith agreed.

One of the gay guys on the bed took out a black bag from his pocket, and from that bag he removed a small plastic tube with ten candies inside. While I was counting out the money, the woman on the floor removed a tray from under the bed. There were two guns and half a dozen empty boats on the tray.

"Smoke here, please," the woman said sweetly.

I placed four candies on the tray and I told Kun that Keith and I wanted to give a candy to each of them. Perhaps it would have been more polite to personally hand each of them a candy, but candies were a dirty drug so we tried not to touch the candy directly with our fingers. Kun looked happy with our decision to share the candy, and when he translated my words for his friends, they all thanked us in chorus. Kun and his friends had welcomed us into their room and they sold candy to us at a really good price, so we were happy to share candy with them.

"I guess 200,000 for ten is the price Lao people pay," I said to Keith.

Keith took the mini gun from his pocket. Kun asked to take a closer look at it. Kun and his three friends looked at the gun in amazement. They had never seen a gun made out of a travel size mouthwash bottle before. They all took turns using Keith's mini gun while Keith used their gun. Keith placed all three of his candies on a boat and started smoking as quickly as he could. Then we heard the most frightening sound you can hear when you are in the middle of a candy session. When there are guns and boats everywhere, and there's a dealer with a bag full of candy in his pocket, the last thing you want to hear is a knock on the door. But that's what we heard. Knock! Knock! Keith and I froze. I looked at the four Lao people to see if there was any cause for concern. They all looked worried. Kun called out something in Lao. A woman replied. I suddenly felt at ease because I knew that it wasn't the police. I hid the boat and the gun under the bed while Kun opened the door for his friend. The woman that came in was much older than the rest of us, and, to be honest, she looked homeless. Her hair was frizzy, her clothes were shabby, and she just looked a bit wild. She greeted us and then she used the bathroom without closing the door. When she joined us, I placed one of my candies on the tray for her. Two candies were enough for me, and I didn't want her to feel excluded. After all, she was friends of these kind Lao people who had invited me and Keith into their room. She seemed surprised by my gift and she thanked me several times. It was a strange situation for me and Keith to be in, but the nice thing was that we were with Lao people who were not trying to take advantage of us in any way. They never encouraged us to buy more candy or to go out and buy beer for them, nor did they ask for any money for using the room.

I had only finished one of my candies when Keith had smoked all three of his.

"I'm off," he said. "Are you coming?"

"Where you going?" I asked. "It's only 1:20. I thought we were going to Don Chan at two o'clock?"

"I thought we could go for a beer somewhere first. Let's go."

Kun said that I could stay a little longer to finish my candy, so that's exactly what I did. Keith and I arranged to meet at Don Chan at two o'clock. Five minutes after Keith had left, I finished my candy and by then everybody else had finished their candy too. Kun and his four friends cleared away all the boats and guns, and then they opened the door to let in some fresh air. They all stood outside the door and talked together for a few minutes. The bed was empty so I lay down and checked my heart rate. It was very fast, but it was regular. I thought I would be able to close my eyes for a few minutes and give my heart a chance to slow down, but Kun came back into the room and sat next to me on the bed. Without saying anything, he placed his hand on my leg. I removed it immediately and I told him that I am not gay.

"You have three options," he started. "I like you, but my two friends like you too - the two women. I go with you for free, the old lady go with you for free, or you can go with the young woman, but you pay her 50,000 kip. What you want?"

He placed his hand on my leg again, but I removed it straight away and I thought for a moment about the options he outlined. The problem was that the young woman was very plain looking, and the older woman looked terrible. Until Kun had come back into the room, I had no desire to be with either of these women. My plan was to go to Don Chan and hook up with a woman there. I didn't have many chances to go to Don Chan without Fon, so I planned to make the most of the night. I looked at the time on my phone. It was 1:30. I decided to pay the 50,000 kip (five dollars) and fool around with the young woman for fifteen minutes and then leave for Don Chan. Usually women in Lao try to charge foreigners about 250,000 kip, and then the price can drop if the falang negotiates properly, but I had never heard of a Lao woman charging a falang 50,000 kip. Perhaps she was giving me this price because I had shared candy with her and her friends, or perhaps this is the price Lao men pay.

"So you need to pay 50,000 for the girl and 20,000 for the room," Kun said.

"20,000 kip for this room?" I asked, a little annoyed.

"Not this room," Kun explained. "This my room. You and she need to get room together."

I handed Kun 70,000 kip and a few minutes later the woman came back with towels and a room key. The woman led me to a small, old building behind the main building of the guesthouse. The door was locked with a padlock. When we went inside, I was surprised to see that the floor of the room was bare concrete and there were holes in the ceiling. The woman handed me the towels while she went back to the other room to get a bottle of water from her friends. The bed was just an old, bare grey mattress on a metal frame - not too dissimilar to a bed you might see in a prison. I used the towels to cover some of the dirty mattress. When the woman returned, I asked her, "This room 20,000 for short time?"

"No," she said. "20,000 for one night."

It was the cheapest room I had ever seen in Laos, but then again it was also the worst. I fooled around with the woman for ten minutes to get my money's worth, but I wasn't really interested in her. When we stopped, she agreed to give me a lift to Don Chan on her scooter for 20,000 kip.

Don Chan Palace is a huge luxury hotel on the Mekong River about five minutes away from falang town. Vientiane is a small, under developed city made up of old low-lying buildings and quiet roads. I once heard that there is a law in Laos that says that no building in Vientiane can be higher than the Pha That Luang temple. It is the national symbol of Laos, so this law is designed to preserve the importance of the building. But Don Chan Palace is fourteen stories high. It towers over the rest of the city. Apparently the owners of Don Chan Palace got around the law by building the hotel on an island on the Mekong River. There are a lot of rumors about Don Chan Palace. Many people say that it is owned by mega rich Chinese business men, and even though the hotel makes a loss, they don't care because they only use the hotel to launder dirty money.

I arrived at Don Chan just after two o'clock. I met Keith standing by the elevators in the reception area. He was speaking with a beautiful young Lao woman.

"I'll follow you up in a few minutes, mate," Keith said to me.

There was a nightclub on the eighth floor of Don Chan Palace. I felt a little awkward going to the club on my own. Don Chan's nightclub opened until about three or three-thirty AM, so a lot of Lao women and falang men left Samlo at two o'clock and came to Don Chan. Don Chan was also popular with young Lao men and women who didn't have any interest in falangs. Young people came from all parts of the city to Don Chan because it opened later than any other nightclub. That's why there were always a lot of people that I didn't know in Don Chan. I only knew people from falang town.

I paid 30,000 at the door and I went straight to the bar to get a drink. In Don Chan there was an open-air section where the music was low and the lighting was bright. There was an indoor section too - a dark, air-conditioned club with thumping music and groups of people dancing around small round tables. I sat at the bar in the open area and enjoyed my beer. There were dozens of Lao women that I knew. They were all either walking to and from the bathroom or sitting with falang men at nearby tables. I had only been at the bar a few minutes when a Lao woman that I vaguely recognized approached me.

"I know you," she said, pointing at me and leaning back.

"I know you too, but I'm not sure how," I replied.

"We met on the bus to Bankgok a few months ago."

"Oh! Right!" I exclaimed. Suddenly I remembered her clearly.

Back in April I left Laos and went home for two months. My

flight was from Bangkok, so I took the overnight bus to Bangkok from Vientiane. The woman sitting next to me was this beautiful Lao woman. For the first two hours of that trip I was crying my eyes out. I wasn't ready to leave Fon or Laos. Plus, all the candy that I had smoked and all the sleep that I had missed had made me lose control of my emotions. I'm not sure if this woman had seen me crying or not. If she had two eyes in her head, she must have seen me constantly wiping my tears away. After I stopped crying, we ended up talking for several hours. She was a really sweet girl, and I was jealous that she was going to meet her boyfriend in Kao San Road. Her boyfriend was an English guy who was working as an English teacher in Bangkok. When we arrived in Bangkok, her boyfriend was waiting for her when we got off the bus. She introduced us briefly and then I bid them farewell. It was a nice memory. I guess I had always thought that she had moved to Bangkok and started living with her nice falang boyfriend. She seemed different to the Lao women I had met in falang town. But soon after she came over to talk to me in Don Chan, her new falang came out of the bathroom, so she ended our conversation abruptly. A few minutes later she came back to the bar with her falang, except this time she had to pretend not to know me. Her new falang didn't even know how to count the Lao money and he couldn't remember the girl's name so he kept calling her 'Missy'.

I got a text message from Keith, saying that he was going back to his guesthouse with the girl that he had just met. I was bored standing on my own at the bar so I decided to have a look in the indoor section. As I walked between the groups of young Lao women, I scanned the room to see if there was anybody I knew. That's when I saw Fon standing at a table with her two gay friends, Guy and Tik. There was also a Turkish man named Kadir with them. Kadir's parents owned a Turkish restaurant in falang town. Fon had told me that she was spending the night in her family home, yet here she was dancing and drinking with a falang guy. To make it worse, Fon had once admitted to me that she had slept with Kadir a few months before she hooked up with me. Guy saw me, and when we made eye contact I rushed outside. I went back to the bar. My heart was pumping with rage. Guy followed me to the bar.

"Why you here?" he asked. "Fon say you asleep in home."

"I was asleep but then I got a message from Keith saying that he is back in Laos, so I had to meet up with him."

"Keith from England is back? Crazy Keith?"

"Yeah, English Keith."

"Why you no tell Fon that you come out tonight?"

"It doesn't matter, Guy. We don't need to talk about it," I said, fed up with everything. "Fon can do whatever she wants."

Guy went back inside and a few minutes later Fon came to the bar.

"Why you here?" she asked, on the attack. "You say you sleep."

"As I told Guy, Keith messaged me saying that he is back in Laos, so I agreed to meet him."

"Keith is back?" Fon asked, a little disgusted at the thought. "So you smoke all day with him?"

"I don't want to argue here in public. Just tell me why you are with Kadir."

"He come to our table and start talking with us. What's the problem?"

"You fucked him before! That's the problem!" I said, slamming the beer down on the counter and then I stormed off.

I walked back to my apartment and I called Ting on the way. He was on his way back into Vientiane and he could be at my place in twenty minutes.

After Ting left, I smoked candy on my own for a while, but thoughts of Fon and Kadir ran around my mind over and over again. I called Fon's phone but it just rang out. This added fuel to my imagination. I convinced myself that she was with Kadir. I called her a few more times but the phone kept going to voice mail. At about four o'clock, I called her and this time her phone was turned off. I didn't have Tik or Guy's number, so I had absolutely no way of contacting Fon or finding out where she was. I was sitting at the edge of my sofa tapping my feet constantly and biting my nails in frustration. I called Fon's phone over and over again, and when that failed I searched my contacts desperately for the phone number of somebody that might be able to help me reach her. But I knew that there was nothing I could do until Fon turned her phone back on. I had to wait.

I smoked five candies within a couple of hours and I hid the remaining five candies under the sink in the bathroom. I heated up some green curry and tried to eat some of it, but I couldn't swallow more than a couple of mouthfuls. I didn't want to be alone anymore. I called Keith. He didn't answer my call but he sent me a message a few minutes later asking if he could come to my place to hang out. When Keith arrived, he gave me money for the candy I gave him earlier in the night. Even though I had five candies left, Keith insisted on calling Ting.

"I want to get a big order in," he said. "How much will Ting charge me for 20 candies?"

"440,000, maybe 420,000. He doesn't lower the price much, no matter how much you want to order."

While we waited for Ting, Keith smoked candy and he was excited to tell me about his new girlfriend, Sarah.

"She is so beautiful, isn't she?" he kept saying. "She is breathtaking. And she looks so different to other Lao women."

"Where is she now?" I asked.

"She went back home. She wanted to get home before her kid wakes up."

"She has a kid?"

"Yeah, an eight-year-old girl. She had the kid when she was seventeen. But it gets weirder."

"Go on."

"She still lives with her ex-husband...a falang guy from America."

"And he's the father of the kid?"

"Yes. Sarah hates him, but he wants them all to live together so that he can take care of the kid."

"I don't think he would be too happy if he knew that she stayed with you last night."

"But Sarah hates him," Keith insisted.

"It's a weird situation, mate. Be careful."

"I will, but I can see myself falling in love with this girl."

Keith always seemed to have problems with women. The last time he was in Laos he had a Lao girlfriend who didn't speak any English. Fon and I had to translate for them. One night when we were on our way to Don Chan, Keith spoke to his girlfriend on the phone. He wanted to say 'I am going to Don Chan with my friend' in Lao, but instead he said 'I am going to Don Chan with my fuck buddy.' I burst out laughing when I heard him say this. His girlfriend hung up the phone and she didn't answer his calls for the next few days. The girl knew that Keith couldn't speak Lao well, so surely she knew that it was just an innocent mistake. Anyway, she did well out of it. In the end, she made Keith feel so guilty that he ended up buying her a new phone.

"Does Sarah smoke?" I asked Keith.

"No, and she doesn't know that I smoke either so don't mention anything about candy when you meet her. The only problem is that I know a couple of her mates from Don Chan, and they know that I smoke, so they might tell her."

"It might be difficult to hide it from her for a long time. Are you sure she doesn't smoke? She is very very skinny, right?"

"Actually, I thought she smoked too because she is so slim, but from some of the things she was saying earlier I could tell that she definitely doesn't smoke, and straight after we had sex she fell asleep for an hour. She wouldn't have been able to sleep if she had smoked candy, right? But while she was asleep I was just waiting there for her to wake up and go home so that I could come here and smoke."

Keith and I smoked candy until the morning. At about nine o'clock, Keith got a call from Sarah. She wanted Keith to come collect her from her house.

As Keith was getting ready to leave, we heard a man playing an acoustic guitar and singing a Lao song.

"What is that?" Keith asked.

"There is a prison next door," I said. "Since a few weeks ago, that guy sings every morning at about this time. I guess he is an inmate."

"But it sounds really close," Keith said, in disbelief, because it sounded like the noise was coming from right outside my back door.

I brought Keith to the back door, and as I reached out my hand to touch the wall that was right next to my apartment complex, I told him, "This is the prison wall."

He looked up to the top of the wall and saw a lot of barbed wire.

"You live next to a prison?"

"Yeah."

"That's fucked up!"

As soon as Keith left, I called Fon. This time she answered the phone.

"Where are you?" I asked calmly, carefully listening for any voices in the background.

"Just driving around," Fon replied with a faint voice.

"What do you mean 'just driving around?'"

"I mean, I'm just driving around. I have nowhere to go."

"You should come here. We need to talk."

"I don't want to fight. I'm too tired."

This made my blood boil, but I continued to speak calmly.

"Just come. We need to talk about last night."

"I don't want to talk about last night. Nothing to say. I just want sleep."

"Just come."

Twenty minutes later Fon arrived at my apartment. She was carrying grilled fish and sticky rice that she had bought on the way.

"Let's eat." she said. She looked exhausted.

While Fon was opening the bags of food, I asked her, "Where did you go last night after Don Chan?"

"I went my friend house to play cards," she replied, in a very matter-of-fact way.

"With who?"

"Tik, Guy and some other people you don't know."

"What about Kadir?"

"No, he no go. He only come talk us five minutes in Don Chan and then he go with some other girl."

"I called you but you didn't answer."

"I no see phone."

"But you turned your phone off in the middle of the night."

"No battery. Later I see phone and I charge it, and when I leave my friend room I turn on phone again."

"But why didn't you charge it straight away?"

"I play cards with friends. I no care my phone."

"But surely you knew that I would call you. How could you not hear or feel your phone vibrate when I called you?"

Fon didn't reply. She had given her version of events and she didn't want to talk about it anymore. But I couldn't let this rest.

"I called you at about three o'clock when you would still be in Don Chan, but you didn't answer then."

"I was in Don Chan. Of course I no hear your call."

"But I kept on calling and calling. When you left Don Chan you didn't check your phone?"

"No, I no check."

"What time did you leave Don Chan?"

Fon didn't answer.

"Why didn't you turn on your phone while it was charging in your friend's house? I mean, it must have been charging for about an hour, so why not turn on your phone while it's charging? You hate having your phone turned off. And your mom usually calls you really early in the morning."

Fon didn't reply. She didn't want to talk anymore.

"Fon, what time did you leave Don Chan?" I asked, getting more and more irate. "Fon, tell me, what time did you leave Don Chan?"

"I eat this and then sleep," she said.

"Fuck that! You are not sleeping here. I'm going to Vang Vieng today," I said, without thinking it through.

"Okay. I sleep here. Your rent finish after few days, right?"

"Right, but I'm leaving today. I will call the landlord and ask her to come straight away, and then I'll go get a bus to Vang Vieng."

"No, I need to sleep, Walt," Fon said, suddenly showing some vulnerability.

"You're not sleeping here."

"Look at me. Don't make me go back my family like this, please, Walt. They will know I smoke drug. Look at me. Please don't do this."

"Go back to the room you were in last night," I said, and as I walked to the bathroom I added, "Or I guess he no want you after he fucked you."

When Fon heard this, she picked up her phone and threw it at my head. I ducked and the phone smashed off the wall.

"Why you talk like that, bastard?" Fon screamed. "Why you make me crazy woman?"

Suddenly I didn't need to go to the bathroom anymore. I went to the wardrobe and started packing my things quickly. Fon was breathing heavily and staring at me intensely. She picked up the gun and the boat and she started smoking quickly.

"I call Ting," she shouted. "Give me your phone."

I knew that I had to call the landlady before Ting came. Otherwise I might end up buying more candy, and I might start to forget about what had happened between me and Fon. I might end up staying in Vientiane for another few days, and if I was feeling lazy after a few days I might even pay another month's rent on the room. I wouldn't let that happen this time. I called the landlord and asked her to come by eleven o'clock to collect my key and check the electricity meter. When Ting came, I bought three candies for myself. Fon paid Ting back for the money and the candies that she had gotten from him the night before. Fon also bought ten candies. She said that she had won money playing cards with her friends. Ting and Fon left together before the landlady arrived. They walked out the door without saying a word to me.

5

I didn't plan to stay in Laos for a long time. My original plan was to travel around the world for a year. My mate from Ireland wanted to see Thailand so I spent the first three weeks of my one-year trip hitting all the usual tourist spots like Bangkok and the islands down south. By the end of those three weeks I already knew that I didn't want to spend the rest of the year backpacking. In the previous three years I had backpacked around Italy and France for two weeks, Southeast Asia for two months, India and Nepal for three months and China for two months. I had convinced myself that I was ready for a full year of constantly being on the move, but I was wrong - I couldn't do that anymore. I didn't have the energy for it. In truth, my previous trip around China had killed my passion for travelling. It was a boring trip. So, by the tender age of twenty-three I was all travelled out.

When my friend went back to Ireland I had one week left on my Thai tourist visa. I started looking online for cheap places I could stay for a long time. I figured if I went to a quiet place away from the big tourist spots I could live very cheaply. I wanted to stay in one place for a couple of months and try writing something - some stories or even a book. I didn't really care if it was by a beach, in the mountains or in a city. I just wanted to live as cheaply as I could for a while, write for a few hours a day, relax and enjoy the quiet life. While I was searching online, I found a nice guesthouse in the south of Thailand. It was only a hundred dollars a month and it was right next to a beach. It seemed to be located in quite a remote area, but there was a small store and a restaurant in the guesthouse. It looked perfect for me. I decided I would go stay there as soon as I came back from my visa run to Laos.

I had been to Vientiane a couple of times before, so I was familiar with falang town. I knew a cheap guesthouse on the second road, I knew Samlo was a fun bar, and I knew a great Indian restaurant by the river. After only a few days in Laos, I realized there was no need to go all the way to the south of Thailand for somewhere cheap and comfortable to live. Vientiane would do just fine. I was paying five dollars for a room, but it was a very old building with creaky wooden floors and a shared bathroom. A girl in Samlo recommended another guesthouse on the second road. It was the same price but it had a private bathroom with tiled floors. Suddenly my standard of living went up a notch. I was delighted with my new surroundings. I lived a very simple life in Vientiane. I relaxed during the day and pushed myself to write for an hour before I went out for a late dinner. I went to Samlo every night to drink beer and play pool. I fell into this routine quite easily and the weeks and months flew by.

I lived in Vientiane for six months without even hearing about 'candy' or 'chocolate'. In October, my seventh month in Laos, I was still living in the same guesthouse and I became friends with a Lao girl a few doors down from me. Her name was Gin and she was from Luang Prabang. She said she was staying in Vientiane for a month to sort out a visa to go stay with her boyfriend in Germany. Gin and I got on really well. It was a purely plutonic relationship. We sometimes played pool together during the day and we often went to Samlo together at night. One night after Samlo we started talking to a guy called Simon outside our guesthouse. He was sitting on a bench enjoying a beer, so we joined him and we all got along very well. After that the three of us had a few beers together in Samlo or outside the guesthouse most nights. Simon was an English lad in his early thirties. He always spoke quite vaguely about his past, but from what I could gather he had been in Southeast Asia, mostly Thailand, for about five years, working in bars and any other odd job he could find.

One night in Samlo, Simon casually dropped into the conversation that he smoked candy. Gin understood what he meant by 'candy' straight away, but I didn't have a clue what he was talking about until he reluctantly whispered the word 'yaba' to make me understand. I didn't know anything about yaba at the time. Simon explained that it was known as the 'crazy drug'.

"When people smoke it, they don't sleep or eat for several days at a time," he explained. "Some people go crazy on it. They flip out and do weird shit. It was originally used by truck drivers in Thailand so that they could drive for a long time without stopping to rest, but now it's used by young people."

"Why do you smoke it?" I asked, because it sounded terrible.

"It makes you feel good," he said. "It makes you feel happy and full of energy."

It soon became clear that Simon had serious money problems. One night he told me that he was five weeks behind on his room bill. Simon never asked me for money, but whenever we went to Samlo I paid for his beers. I don't think he ever asked Gin for money either, but one day she gave him 250,000 kip for candy. I was really annoyed when I found out about this.

"Why did you give him money for drugs?"

"Because he need," she said. "I want help him."

"You shouldn't give him money for drugs," I said firmly. "If you want to help him, you should buy him food or pay some of his room bill."

One morning I bumped into Simon in the hallway and he told me that he had just come back from a PC cafe.

"I sent out a few feelers to some of my friends," he said. "Hopefully one of them will send me some money in the next day or two. I told them that I just need enough money for a flight home."

"Do you think someone will send you that much?" I asked.

"I'm not sure. A couple of mates sent me money for a flight before, but I just pissed it up the wall in a week."

That evening Simon came to my room for a chat. He noticed that I had a laptop. He asked to borrow it for the night so that he could watch a movie in his room. I told him that I planned to stay in and watch some TV shows on the laptop on my own, but Simon wouldn't let it drop. He kept pleading with me to lend him the laptop. It was incredibly awkward to keep refusing him, but I could see that something wasn't right. I knew I shouldn't lend him the laptop. The next morning the man at the reception told me that Simon left in the middle of the night without paying his room bill. I never saw him again. The following week Gin returned to Luang Prabang to get more documents for her visa. I was alone again.

A few days after Gin went back to Luang Prabang, I was drinking alone in Samlo and a girl I had never seen before caught my eye. She had long curly black hair and she was wearing a very revealing green dress. She looked a little different to other Lao women. I was sitting at the bar on my own and she was sitting at a table with a friend. We made eyes at each other a few times, but neither of us made a move. I didn't like picking up women in Samlo because I knew too many people there. When Samlo closed at two o'clock, she left with her friend. I didn't want to go back to my guesthouse alone. I wanted to find the woman in the green dress. It was raining quite heavily outside so I was worried that she might have just gone straight back to her room with her friend. Most of these Lao women rode scooters, so they didn't like to stay out in the rain. The only hope I had of finding her would be in the night club in Don Chan Palace. I got a tuk-tuk straight there, but when I was walking through the reception area I noticed that it was very quiet. When I stepped out of the elevator, a security man told me the club was closing early. There weren't any customers because of the rain so there was no point keeping the club opened. The tuk-tuk driver was waiting for me in the car park. I asked him to bring me back to falang town, but on the way back another tuk-tuk passed us and I saw the girl I liked in the back of the tuk-tuk with her friend. She started gesturing for me to come to her. I told the tuk-tuk driver to stop. I paid the tuk-tuk driver the full fare and I jumped into the back of the other tuk-tuk with the two women.

The girl in the green dress was called Jib, and her friend's name was Kung. They brought me to a rundown guesthouse outside falang town. As soon as we got into the room, Kung started looking for things under the bed, and Jib started rummaging through her bag in the corner. I stood back and watched while I dried myself off with a towel. Kung sat on the floor and started smoking something through a water bottle (which I now know was a gun).

"What is that?" I asked Kung.

"Candy. Yaba," she said. "Come, come."

Normally I might have hesitated or even refused her offer, but I was drunk, and, to be honest, I had been curious about candy ever since Simon had told me about it. I sat down at the edge of the bed in front of Kung.

"I do for you. One moment," she said, as she took off her wet hoodie.

Under the hoodie Kung was wearing a revealing red and black striped dress. She knelt down in front of me and handed me the gun.

"You hold this," she said sweetly. "I burn for you."

Kung had to lean forward to burn the candy for me, so I had a great view of her cleavage. Her breasts were huge. I had never seen breasts that size in Laos or Thailand before. As I inhaled the candy I stared blatantly at her breasts. When I looked up at Kung, she smiled back at me. She wanted me to look. She leaned forward more so that I would have a better view.

"You like my friend?" she asked.

"Yes, I guess so," I said awkwardly.

Jib was sitting right behind her making another gun. I smoked more candy and looked at her breasts again. Jib finished making her gun, so she sat next to me on the bed and burned the candy for me. It was much more exciting when Kung did it.

"Actually, I really like your friend," I told Jib. "Is that okay?"

"Yes, no problem," she said. "You like me, my friend, both of us, everything okay. No worry."

Kung burnt the candy for me again. As I was inhaling the candy slowly and looking down at her huge breasts, she kept saying very softly, "I take good care you. I take good care man."

A few minutes later all the candy was gone. I felt great. I felt alive. I was so happy to be with these two women. I had only known Jib and Kung for about twenty minutes but I suddenly felt very close to them. I was feeling very positive about everything. Also, I didn't feel drunk anymore. The candy had sobered up my mind and body. But the feeling was not as strong as I had expected. I thought I needed to smoke more to get the full benefits of candy

"Can we order more?" I asked them.

"Yes, you want?"

"Yes. I will pay."

"Okay. I call my friend now," Kung said.

While we were waiting for their friend to come, I took out 500,000 kip from my wallet and handed them 250,000 each. I was feeling very generous all of a sudden.

"Why?" Kung asked, pleasantly surprised to be handed free money.

"I just want you to have it," I said. "Why not?"

Their friend (who turned out to be Ting) came to the room and I bought ten candies from him. He came to our room every couple of hours through the night and into the morning. I planned to go home at midday, but I didn't want to go out in the sun, so I asked Kung and Jib if I could stay until the evening. When the sun went down I decided to smoke more to get me through the night, but after I smoked I didn't want to go back to my guesthouse alone. I stayed with Kung and Jib, and we smoked together until the next morning. I kept smoking to get back the happy feeling I had at the start, but it never came. All the joy and excitement that had been rushing through my veins had now turned to a kind of numbness and indifference to everything. In the early morning Kung went out to get breakfast from a restaurant nearby. While she was gone, Jib confessed that they had stolen money from my wallet while I was in the shower. She seemed genuinely sorry. I checked my wallet. There was a hundred dollars missing. I didn't feel any anger or resentment towards her.

"No problem," I said. "I would have given you both money anyway. I had a really good time."

When Kung came back, I said goodbye and went back to my own room in falang town. It took me a few days to catch up on all the sleep and meals I had missed. I was glad that I had tried candy, but I had no interest in trying it ever again. I couldn't understand how Simon had been so addicted to it. It made me feel very happy when I first smoked it, and it made sex amazing, but apart from that the effect wasn't very strong. I mean, when I imagined the effects of drugs like heroin and cocaine, candy seemed like a kind of weak drug in comparison. I certainly couldn't imagine myself ever craving it.

A few days after my candy session with Jib and Kung, I went to Samlo for the first time in almost a week. I talked with Sit, I played pool, and as the place filled up I chatted away to whoever sat next to me at the bar. I thought everything was back to normal, but then a Lao woman I knew called Sky came up to me and whispered, "Why you no smoke with me?"

"What are you talking about?" I asked, planning to deny everything.

"I hear you smoke with two women in guesthouse."

"Who told you?"

"Next time you want smoke, ask me. We friends long time."

Over the next few days several other women and ladyboys that I knew came up to me in Samlo and said they heard that I had smoked. I felt really uncomfortable with this because I didn't want Sit and the other workers in Samlo to think that I used candy.

One night I drank a little more than usual in Samlo, and when the bar closed, instead of going back to my room, I started wandering around the streets of falang town. I wasn't ready to go back to my room and sleep yet. Down one of the side streets I saw Sky sitting on her motorbike. I guessed she was looking for a customer.

"Walt, what you doing?" she asked.

"I want to smoke," I said.

I'm not sure why I suddenly wanted to smoke candy when I was drunk. I guess I was bored and lonely, so doing drugs with a beautiful woman in the middle of the night appealed to me. Sky brought me to her room in a cheap guesthouse at the end of the street. She knocked on one of the rooms and when the door opened I saw five Lao women sitting on the floor smoking candy. I knew all five of them from Samlo. Sky bought ten candies from her friend with my money, and then we headed to my guesthouse to smoke. We smoked for two nights and two days.

The candy session with Sky was a lot of fun, but I regretted it because I was worried that I was getting hooked on candy. When I was sober, I had no interest in the stuff, but twice in the space of a week I had gotten drunk and ended up smoking it. It was becoming a problem. Alcohol was weirdly becoming a gateway drug. I decided to only drink two or three beers a night for a while until I got through this phase. It worked. I didn't get drunk or smoke candy for the next few weeks. The interesting thing was that now that I knew a little bit about candy, I started to see some things differently. For example, I suddenly understood why some of the Lao women and ladyboys in falang town were very underweight. I used to put this down to genetics or to not having enough money for food, but now I was sure that it was because of candy. I also remembered that ladyboys (mainly in Thailand, not so much in Laos) were notoriously aggressive and unpredictable, even to falangs passing by on the street, and I figured that was probably because of candy too.

Now that I was only drinking a couple of beers a night, I didn't give much thought to candy. Then one night Ted sat down next to me in Samlo. I had not seen him in almost three months. We drank a lot and I told him that I had tried candy a couple of times recently.

"Have you ever tried it?" I asked him.

"Of course I have," he said. "I have some in my room. Let's go smoke a few now before we go to Don Chan."

A few days later I checked out of my guesthouse, left most of my stuff in the guesthouse's storage room and got on an overnight bus to Bangkok. I needed to get away from candy for a while. I stayed in a guesthouse near Kao San Road and I did some things that I couldn't do in Vientiane, like watching a movie in the cinema and going to McDonalds. It was nice to be in a big city again. But I chose the wrong city to get away from drugs. One night I got drunk at an alcohol cart near Nana Plaza and I told one of the workers that I wanted to smoke candy. Within half an hour I was in her room smoking ice – that's all she could find at such short notice. It was much more expensive than candy, but it had a very similar effect. I returned to Laos the following week and I vowed not to get drunk again for a while. I stayed in my old guesthouse for one night, but the next day I moved into an apartment right next to Namphu Fountain. It only cost one hundred and twenty dollars a month, and it was much bigger than my old room. It had a TV, a kitchen and it even had air conditioning. My standard of living jumped up a notch again. By this time, I wasn't writing anymore. I had given up. The stories I had written during my first six months in Laos were all terrible, but the problem now was that I didn't have anything more I wanted to write about. I used to walk around falang town in the evenings trying to think of interesting plots and characters, but I was all out of ideas. My life in Laos was still good, but I was starting to wonder if it was time to move on. And then one day Guy stopped me on the street with a proposition.

One Saturday afternoon in early December I went for lunch in Noi's Restaurant as usual, and right after that I went to a PC café to check what soccer matches were scheduled that day. I always watched soccer matches in Samlo on Saturday and Sunday nights. There was an early kick-off that day, so I planned to go to Samlo at eight-thirty PM. After I checked the soccer fixtures, I started walking back to my apartment. When I passed Khop Chai Deu, a young Lao guy that I had never met before stood in front of me and said, "Hi, how are you?"

Just from that one question alone I guessed that he was gay because his voice was very effeminate.

"I'm good, thanks," I said, with my head down as I walked around him.

He started walking with me.

"Where you go?" he asked.

"Sorry, I'm not interested."

"Wait, wait," he said. "Your name is Walt, right? I heard you smoke."

This caught my attention. We both stopped walking. I wanted to know how this complete stranger knew my name and why he was coming up to me on the street in broad daylight and talking to me about candy.

"What are you talking about?" I asked, already irritated.

"My name is Guy. I am a friend of Kung and Jib," he said, with a big smile.

Guy's head was perfectly round and it looked like he had two big balls on his cheekbones when he smiled.

"So what?" I said.

"So I know you smoke sometimes."

"I gotta go home now, sorry."

"Wait, I want to ask you something."

"What?"

"Me and my friends want to smoke tonight but we have nowhere to go. I thought maybe we can come to your apartment and smoke with you."

"My apartment? No, no, sorry. Just go to a guesthouse."

I started to walk off again. Guy followed me.

"Wait, it might be fun. Maybe you will like my friend. She is really beautiful and glamorous."

By now we were next to Namphu Fountain. I didn't want to lead Guy any closer to my apartment, so I had to stand with him and bring the conversation to an end in that spot.

"Why don't you just go to a guesthouse to smoke like everybody else?"

"My friend doesn't like to go to those kinds of guesthouses. She is from a kind of rich family. She is kind of high class."

This surprised me. I didn't know how to respond.

"And she has a car," Guy added, "so she doesn't want to park it outside a guesthouse."

"Your friend owns a car?" I asked, astonished.

"Yes, she has quite a new car. I told you, she is from a good family. Maybe you will like her."

I was intrigued. I wanted to meet this girl. But I didn't want to do candy and I didn't want complete strangers smoking in my apartment. I hesitated for a while.

"She has money. She will buy candy for you. You don't need to pay," Guy assured me.

"I don't want to smoke," I said. "If you and your friend come to my apartment, I won't smoke."

"Okay, No problem. We can smoke and when we are finished we can all go to Don Chan together."

"How many friends?"

"Just me, one girl and one other boy."

"How old is the girl?"

"24."

"Oh! Same as me. Can she speak English?"

"Yes, she has amazing English. Don't worry. You will like her. Many falangs like her."

"Okay. So what time?" I asked, a little tentatively, a little excited.

"My friend likes to start smoking at about nine o'clock. Is that okay?

We agreed that Guy and his two friends would come to my place at nine o'clock.

As I walked back to my apartment, I was in shock. I couldn't believe what had just happened. I had agreed to let three complete strangers come smoke candy in my place. The more I thought about it, the more I started to regret it. It seemed like a really dangerous situation. It could be a set up by the police, or Guy and his friends could have a plan to steal my stuff or trick me out of money. I considered just going to Samlo at eight-thirty PM like I originally planned so that my apartment would be empty when Guy and his friends arrived. But after I thought about it some more, I decided to keep my agreement with Guy. I figured that as long as I didn't smoke candy everything would be okay. Plus, I really wanted to meet the girl.

I cleaned my apartment in the evening, and on my way back from an early dinner in Noi's restaurant I bought a few big bottles of Beer Lao and some ice in a nearby store. I made sure to shower and dress nicely. I watched the start of the soccer match while I was waiting for Guy and his friends to arrive. I was nervous. A few minutes after nine o'clock I saw the bright headlights of a car shine through my front window. I opened the door to welcome my guests. The car was small, but it looked shiny and new. First Guy and his gay friend, Tik, stepped out of the car. I shook their hands and welcomed them into my apartment. I waited at the door for the girl. When she finally got out of the car I was a little surprised by her appearance. She wasn't glamorous at all. She was wearing jeans and a simple black T-shirt. But she was pretty and she looked really cool with dark, heavy eye makeup. Her hair was dark brown and shoulder length, and it was still a little wet from a shower she must have had right before she came out. We

118

shook hands in the doorway and she smiled at me brightly.

"Thanks for letting us come here," she said.

She looked a little uncomfortable. I think she realized that this was a weird situation.

"What's your name?" I asked.

"Fon."

I closed the door and the curtains. There were only two chairs in the living room so I suggested that they go into my bedroom to smoke. Fon and I sat at the edge of the bed while Guy and Tik sat on the floor. Fon took out ten candies from her bag. Guy started making boats while Tik and Fon both made a gun each. We all talked while they were busy making stuff.

"You smoke?" Tik asked me.

"I smoked a couple of times," I said. "But I don't want to smoke this time."

"Why not?" he asked.

"I just don't want to," I said, shrugging my shoulders instead of giving a specific reason.

"No problem," Fon said kindly. "You no want to smoke, you no smoke. That good."

They all started smoking and I just sat and watched. Guy and Tik kept offering me candy but I kept refusing. After about an hour, their friend, Ting, dropped by briefly and Fon bought ten more candies. I was impressed by Fon. She had a car, she had money, and apparently she was from a good family.

There were three people smoking candy in my bedroom, so it took a lot of will power to not join in. As well as instantly giving you a rush and making you feel happy, the actual action of smoking candy was enjoyable because it was usually done in groups and it tasted really nice. After a couple of hours I gave in and I decided to smoke with them. Ting dropped by again. Fon offered to pay, but I insisted on paying this time. Before the ten candies were gone, Guy and Tik went out somewhere for a while. Perhaps they were giving me and Fon a chance to hook up, but at the time I thought Fon was so high class and sophisticated that she would be disgusted by me if I made a move on her so soon. So, we just chilled out and talked in the bedroom. Fon said that she didn't have a job because her family supported her. This seemed to support Guy's claim that Fon was high class and from a rich family. I told Fon that I went to Samlo every night but that I had never seen her there. She said she never went to those kinds of falang bars. She only liked to go to the club in Don Chan sometimes because she liked to dance. At about one o'clock Guy and Tik came back and we all set out for Don Chan Palace in Fon's car. We turned the music in the car on full blast and off we went. I had never been in a car in Laos before. It sure beat going to Don Chan in a crappy tuk-tuk. I felt good when I stepped out of the car with Fon in the Don Chan car park. I felt different to other falangs because this girl was not a normal Lao girl. I felt proud to be with her.

It was a fun night in Don Chan. I stayed close to Fon the whole night. We made a lot of eye contact and I touched her on the small of her back a few times to show her that I liked her. At three-thirty Fon and I left the club holding hands. We had sex that night and amazingly we both managed to get some sleep. It was nice to wake up the next morning with Fon by my side. I had never had a girlfriend in Laos. It felt good. Right after she woke up, Fon called Ting. I went out to eat breakfast while she waited for him. I couldn't understand why she wanted to smoke candy right after she woke up. When I went back to my apartment after breakfast, Tik and Guy were smoking in the bedroom with Fon. I refused to join in for a while, but in the end I gave in again. Tik and Guy left after a few hours, but Fon stayed.

I seemed to become addicted to candy within a week. It was a fun drug to do. It tasted good and it made me happy. And it was amazing how candy fitted every situation. When Fon and I had a fight, we knew that candy would calm us down and make us feel better. When we were happy, we wanted to smoke to keep the good feeling going. When we were bored, candy helped pass the time away. Sometimes I tried to stop for a few days, but then Fon would smoke right in front of me and I couldn't resist. Other times Fon wanted to take a break, but then I would call Ting, and Fon would end up smoking with me. There was no escape for either of us when we were together.

6

It is a long, straight, bumpy road from Vientiane to Vang Vieng. I got a seat on one of the V.I.P. tourist buses in the afternoon, but I knew in advance that it would just be a standard mini bus. Every tourist bus in Southeast Asia seems to be labeled a V.I.P. bus. I sat on a narrow, single seat by the window. I kept the window open to let in a cool breeze. The mini bus didn't have air conditioning so everybody was happy for me to leave the window open. Before I could close my eyes and get some rest, I messaged Keith to tell him that I was going to Vang Vieng for a while, and then I turned off my phone. I knew that as long as my phone was off I would have some peace.

I found myself surrounded by backpackers for the first time in a long time. I was surrounded by about a dozen of them. They were all in their twenties and they were all from either Europe or North America. Two guys that were traveling together fell asleep as soon as the bus set off, and three American girls were talking quite loudly about how boring their time in Vientiane had been and about how much they planned to drink in Vang Vieng. But every so often they reminded themselves that they would go sightseeing and try to experience the culture in the town too. Of course they also talked about going tubing. Tubing was the main attraction in Vang Vieng. Falangs rented large, black inflatable tubes and floated down the river. There were dozens of bars dotted along the river, so the falangs stopped off at bars along the way and got very drunk, and there were drugs on offer too. Tubing seemed to be getting more and more popular every year. A lot of young backpackers from around the world were coming to Laos specifically to experience tubing in Vang Vieng.

Vang Vieng is a tiny town located one hundred and fifty-seven kilometers north of Vientiane. The government continues to improve the road to Vang Vieng, but it still takes about four hours to get there. Vang Vieng might be the strangest place I have ever been to. When I first visited Vang Vieng as a twenty-year-old backpacker, my first impression was that it was just a couple of paved roads in the middle of nowhere, with the sole purpose of hosting foreigners. All the restaurants played back-to-back episodes of the TV show 'Friends' from early in the morning until late at night. As you walked along the street you could hear canned laughter coming from everywhere, and every couple of minutes you could hear the 'Friends' theme tune. People started calling Vang Vieng 'Friends Town'. Backpackers would go into these restaurants and watch 'Friends' for several hours while they ate fried rice and drank milkshakes. People didn't have smart phones and tablet PCs back then, and most backpackers stayed in guesthouses that didn't have any TV, so backpackers didn't have many chances to watch TV during their travels. Vang Vieng was like the rest station in the Southeast Asian backpacking scene. It was a place to stop and take a breather.

But there were weird things to be found in Vang Vieng. A lot of the restaurants had a 'special' section on the menu. 'special' meant 'marijuana'. You could order 'special pizza' and 'special milkshakes', but you could also order magic mushrooms and opium. It was written on the back of the menus in a lot of the restaurants in Vang Vieng. The last time I had visited Vang Vieng, Fon and I went to a bar to buy candy from the owner. While we were waiting at the bar, I started talking to an English guy.

"What are you buying?" I asked him.

"Heroin," he replied simply.

"Can you buy that here?" I asked, shocked.

"Yeah, it's here on the menu," he said, holding up the 'special menu' to me, and on it was written 'Heroin', directly under 'Yaba'.

I was stuck in a shitty mini bus with twelve backpackers, but I felt so different to them. I felt kind of superior to them because I had been living in Laos for a long time and I had been to Vang Vieng before. But in another sense I was jealous because they were moving around from town to town, country to country with their friends, having fun and looking for new experiences, whereas I had somehow become stuck in Laos. They were full of anticipation and wonder about Vang Vieng, yet I was only going to Vang Vieng to rest and spend time on my own. They were making the most of life. I was wasting it.

During the bus ride, my body felt quite good. I was happy closing my eyes and feeling the cool breeze against my face. My heart rate wasn't too bad and I was comforted by the idea that I could sleep for as long as I wanted when I arrived in Vang Vieng. I seemed to keep my eyes shut for the entire bus journey, but there was no danger of me sleeping because of the candy that I had smoked a few hours earlier. I had no interest in listening to music or reading a book. I was happy just to rest. It had been a long time since I felt so at ease. After three and a half hours, we arrived in Vang Vieng. We were lucky to be dropped off in the middle of the town. Often tourists are dropped off a couple of kilometers outside of the town, and then they have to pay the local tuk-tuk drivers to bring them into the centre – a clever trick to get money from falangs.

I couldn't carry my backpack far, so I decided to stay in the guesthouse that I had stayed in with Fon earlier in the year. It took me one minute to walk there. Vang Vieng is a very small town, not too dissimilar to one of those towns in old western movies. Fon brought me to a certain guesthouse before because she said that the owners are her distant relatives so they always give her a discount.

"Only 50,000 kip one night," Fon said to me. "Very good price. Usually 80 or 90,000."

The rooms were quite basic, with a tiny cube TV in the corner. I had already been to Vang Vieng a couple of times on my own so I suggested that this type of room would never cost 80,000 kip.

"You don't know," she told me strongly. "This guesthouse very clean and safe and popular. Not same other guesthouse. 50,000 very good price, good discount. Trust me."

Now that I was going to the guesthouse without Fon, I was interested to see what price they would charge.

"50,000," the owner said, without even looking at me.

"How much if I stay ten nights?" I asked.

125

"You pay ten nights now?"

"Yes, if the price is good."

"Okay. You pay ten nights, it 40,000 one night."

I paid for the ten nights and brought my backpack to my new room. I lay on the bed for a few minutes and tried to think why Fon would have lied to me about getting a discount. Perhaps the guesthouse owners pay Lao women a fee if they bring falang to the guesthouse, or perhaps there was a different reason why Fon wanted to stay only in that guesthouse. I couldn't figure it out.

I wanted to go to bed straight away and sleep as much as I could, but first I had to buy some water. I walked to a small store around the corner. It was about five o'clock in the evening and the streets were quiet. There were a couple of falangs in each of the restaurants along the main street. Only a couple of the restaurants were showing 'Friends'. The other restaurants were showing other popular TV shows like 'The Office' and 'Family Guy'. This was disappointing to see. Vang Vieng seemed like a more unique town when its restaurants played only 'Friends' all day. I bought a bottle of water and a carton of milk in the store and headed back to my room. It was nice to be back in Vang Vieng. I wanted to have a look around to see if it had changed much, but I was only fit for bed.

I fell asleep at about six o'clock that day and I woke up at three AM. I was starving and I was craving cola. I knew that there wouldn't be any restaurant opened at this time, but with any luck there might be a sandwich stall and a small store still open. In Vang Vieng, Lao women set up stalls at the side of the road and sell sandwiches and crepes to falang throughout the day and night. Vang Vieng looked very different at night. All the restaurants were closed and there were perhaps a hundred falangs along the street, but they were gathered in groups in front of these sandwich and crepes stalls. From what I could see, all the falangs were drunk. While I queued up to get my sandwich, a guy started to talk to me in drunken gibberish. I didn't want anything to do with him or the other falangs. I just wanted to be alone. I got my crepe and sandwich and I left quickly. I was fortunate that there was still a store open so I could buy more water, a bag of ice and two big bottles of cola. At the counter I saw lighters and cigarette. If I bought them I would have everything I would need to make a boat and a gun. I contemplated it for a moment. But no, I didn't need any of that stuff now. Plus, the beauty of Vang Vieng was that even if I suddenly had the urge to buy candy, I wouldn't even know where to buy it for a normal price. If I tried to buy it from one of the restaurants, it would probably cost me 100,000 for one, about four times the normal price. I couldn't afford to buy candy at that price. It just wasn't an option for me. Plus, I was too scared to go into a restaurant and order candy and then bring it back to my room and smoke it on my own. What if somebody saw me and followed me back to my room? It was too dodgy. Anyway, now that I was alone in another town, I didn't even have the urge to smoke. To be honest, all I craved was to eat a lot and drink cola, and that's exactly what I did when I got back to my room. In fact, that's all I did for the next few days. I slept, ate and drank. For the first few days in Vang Vieng I could only stay awake for a few hours at a time.

During my second day in Vang Vieng I bought a speaker, so I spent my waking hours listening to music and podcasts in my room on my Mp3 player. My heart was working normally and I wasn't twitching or moving my hands constantly like I tended to do when I was on candy. I was thinking logically and I was reflecting on things calmly. I enjoyed the comfort of the bed and the cool breeze of the ceiling fan. I got all my clothes washed so I felt clean and refreshed. I was getting my strength back so I was able to ejaculate easily. Food tasted good, and even though I was eating a lot and drinking a lot of cola, I was only spending about 150,000 kip a day. I went to an internet café every day to read the football news. I watched football some evenings on my small TV. I kept my phone at the bottom of my bag and I never even considered taking it out and turning it on. The only bad thing about coming off candy was that I was a bit constipated. There is a lot of caffeine in candy, so when you smoke, it completely cleans out your insides. Because of the constipation and the sudden increase in calories, I was getting a small pot belly.

I had originally planned to stay in Vang Vieng for a couple of weeks and then spend my last month in Vientiane, but I was enjoying being alone so much that I started to reconsider this plan. Money was also an issue. If I stayed alone and lived this kind of peaceful life in Vang Vieng or in some other town in Laos, I could make my money go a long way, but if I started smoking again with Fon, I would be out of money long before my flight back to Ireland. When I was in Vientiane with Fon, there were plenty of days when I smoked about twenty candies on my own, but I guess on average Fon and I smoked about thirty candies a day between us. Then, when you factor in accommodation, beer, water, and the odd meal, you're talking about a daily budget of about a hundred dollars. In Vang Vieng, if I ate normally, I could live comfortably on twelve dollars a day – that's a big difference. Now that my body had fully rested, my main purpose of staying in Vang Vieng was to save money but it also occurred to me that I could save just as much money if I used my last month to travel around Laos. The problem was that there wasn't really anywhere else I wanted to go in Laos. I had visited Laos two times on my previous travels, but except for Vientiane and Vang Vieng the only other places I had been to were Luang Prabang, Don Det and a few small towns near the Laos-China boarder. Luang Prabang was impressive because it was a town filled and surrounded by beautiful well-preserved temples, but I didn't fancy the seven-hour bus ride up north on a bumpy road. Don Det is one of four thousand islands on the Mekong River in the very south of Laos. On the island there were about a dozen guesthouses made up of several wooden huts. There weren't any motorbikes or cars on the island because it was so small. The electricity was turned off at nine PM, but at night the bars and restaurants lit their premises with lamps to attract falangs to come and drink beer. It was an interesting experience, but I had no interest in going back there again. There's a city in the south of Laos called Pakse that I had never been to, and a famous prehistoric site called the Plain of Jars that I had always been curious about. However, in the end I decided that for my last month I didn't want to stay somewhere new. I wanted to spend the rest of my time in Vang Vieng and Vientiane. In truth, I fantasized about going back to Vientiane as a single man. There were a lot of beautiful women in Samlo and Don Chan. I figured if I could stay away from Fon I would be able to smoke less candy, go out more and meet a lot of new people. I decided to relax in Vang Vieng for a little while longer and then head back to Vientiane to have some fun. That was my plan for my last month, but things rarely go to plan in Laos.

During my sixth evening in Vang Vieng I went out to eat in an Indian restaurant, and on my way back to my guesthouse I saw a small green car parked in front of my guesthouse. It looked like Fon's car. I peeped through the window and I saw Fon's red hoodie. She knew that I had stayed in Vang Vieng before on my own and that I had stayed in three different guesthouses during those visits. So, there was no way for her to know that I would come back to this guesthouse. *Perhaps she doesn't know that I am staying in this guesthouse,* I thought. *Perhaps she came here with somebody secretly.*

I started walking along the hall of the first floor to see if I could hear her voice from inside one of the rooms, but I could only hear falangs speaking English. I tried the second floor, but there was no sign of her. I looked out over the balcony. I spotted Fon walking along the main street towards the guesthouse. She had a plastic bag in her hand. I ran down the stairs to meet her before she got to her room.

Fon wasn't at all surprised to see me. In fact, I don't recall her even raising her head to look at me. She just stared blankly at the ground as she walked towards her room.

"When did you get here?" I asked, annoyed that Fon was intruding on my peaceful life in Vang Vieng.

"Why you care?" she replied, with blank eyes and a distant voice.

"Don't worry. I know you come here to be alone. I no bother you."

"How did you know I was in this guesthouse?"

Fon didn't answer, but it suddenly occurred to me that she had probably given my name to the guy at reception to see if I was staying there.

I followed Fon. Her room was two doors down from mine. I saw that there was water, cigarettes and three lighters in the plastic bag.

"You'll smoke?" I asked, with mixed emotions.

"Why you care? You come here to rest, so rest."

"You have candy?"

"Only a little."

"How many?"

"Three."

I didn't even consider walking away. I instinctively followed Fon into her room and we smoked the three candies together. Before we even finished the first candy, I started asking her about where we could buy more.

"I don't know. Ask Neung. She come here with me today. Maybe she know where to buy. She party in Vang Vieng many time before."

Neung was Fon's close friend. She was Keith's friend's ex-girlfriend.

"Where is she now?" I asked.

"I don't know. She go to bar near river. Call her if you want buy candy. And Keith come here yesterday. Neung say Keith call you many time but you no answer."

"I'll call Keith when I go out to buy candy.

Fon took two plastic bags out of her backpack and placed them on the bed. She took a new bottle of perfume from one bag and two new T-shirts out of the other bag.

"But I don't understand. Where did you get money to come to Vang Vieng, pay for a guesthouse, buy candy, perfume and clothes?"

"My brother get paid big money this week so he give me three hundred dollars."

According to Fon, her brother was a lawyer and he had just been paid a large lump sum for a big case that he was in charge of. I listened to all this with a pinch of salt.

After we smoked the three candies, I went back to my room to get my phone and I had to use the bathroom because of all the caffeine I had inhaled. Fon counted out 350,000 kip for candy. We argued about who should go to buy the candy, but in the end Fon refused to go. She knew that I had not smoked in five days and that I was desperate. She won.

When I came out of the guesthouse, the main street with all the restaurants that played 'Friends' and other Western sitcoms was to my right. I walked in the opposite direction, towards the river. Every few meters I passed a restaurant or a street stall with three large handwritten standalone menus in front of the entrance – one menu for pancakes, one for sandwiches and one for burgers. As I walked along the street, I wondered where all the local Lao people ate. Surely they don't like pancakes.

It was 9 PM but there weren't many people out yet. Most people would have come back from tubing a couple of hours previous, so they were probably having a power nap before they started drinking again. There were a few young falang couples walking along the street eating pancakes, and a few lone travelers looking for a good place to eat or drink. My mate, Ted, used to refuse to come to Vang Vieng because he said he didn't want to hang out with people half his age. He had a point. All the falangs in Vang Vieng seemed to be backpackers under thirty.

To get to the riverside, I had to turn onto a narrow-paved road. Tuk-tuks and motorcycles sometimes drove along this narrow road, but it was mainly for pedestrians. There were several nice restaurants with wooden decking that hung right over the river. Past those restaurants there were a few dimly lit bars with pool tables and Western music playing loudly. Fon had given me the name of a bar where Neung often bought candy for a good price, but when I went there, the Lao woman behind the bar told me that the owner was away for a few hours. There were a few other falangs in the bar, but, as subtly as I could, I told her that I wanted to buy candy. She said that I would have to wait until the owner came back. She only had marijuana and opium behind the bar. According to Fon, Neung was in one of the bars near the river. I wanted to call Neung to ask about where I could buy candy, but I didn't want to have this conversation on the street. There is a really old, narrow suspension bridge in Vang Vieng that connects to a small river island with several bars. I headed in that direction. On the way there I turned on my phone. I had a dozen messages from Keith. He had arrived in Vang Vieng the previous day. I decided to buy candy before contacting him. I called Neung from the middle of the bridge. There was nobody in sight.

"Neung, this is Walt. Fon and I want to buy candy. I went to the bar you told Fon about, but the owner wasn't there. Do you know any other place I can buy it at a good price?"

"Why you ask me, Walt? Just go to any bar and order. I with friends now," she said, and then she hung up.

What a bitch! I must have given her about thirty candies since the start of the year, and that was the thanks I got. Now I was in a shit position. I didn't know any dealer that I could call, and if I went to a normal bar and tried to buy candy, I would have to pay crazy tourist prices. I called Keith.

"I'm in Space Bar," he said.

I got there in two minutes. It was an open-air bar with a DJ booth and several low wooden platforms spread out around a field. These platforms were covered in rugs for falangs to sit on. The bar looked shit when I arrived because it was empty – it just looked like a field with a few wooden platforms. It was too early in the night. Usually falangs went to the bars in the town early in the night and then moved onto the riverside bars after midnight. Keith and a young Lao guy named Jack were standing at the DJ box playing dance music.

"Where the fuck have you been?" Keith asked. "I've been calling and messaging you."

"My phone was off," I said. "I just wanted to stay away from everything."

"You look much better, healthier. You know Fon is in Vang Vieng, right?"

"I know. We just smoked candy together. She gave me money to buy more, but it's proving difficult."

"How many do you want to buy? Ten?"

"Yeah, ten."

Keith turned to his Lao friend, Jack, and asked him whether his boss would be able to sell me candy for the same price that he sold to Keith. Jack hesitated.

"Not same price," Jack said to Keith. "You special customer. Boss no sell that price to normal falang."

I spoke with Jack in Lao and I told him that I wanted to buy ten candy now but I would be back for another ten candy in the early morning.

"Okay. You buy twenty candy now. I give you good price."

"Sorry. I can only buy ten candies now."

I didn't want to walk back to my guesthouse with twenty candies in my pocket. I had once heard that if the police catch you with more than ten candies they can charge you for possession with intent to distribute, so the most I ever bought was ten.

"Okay. No problem," Jack finally agreed. "You friend of Keith, so I sell you 350,000 kip for ten. No problem."

I counted out the money for him discretely. I invited Keith to smoke with me and Fon, but he wanted to mess around with the DJ equipment for a while. He fancied himself as a DJ. Plus, there was a gun in the bathroom next to the DJ set, so he could smoke there whenever he wanted to.

I had never walked along the street with candy on me before, so on my way back to the guesthouse I was terrified. It was only about a three-minute walk from the riverside bar to the guesthouse, but I was worried that somebody had seen me buy the candy and that they would stop me on the street or follow me back to the guesthouse. I didn't want to hide the candy in my shoe again in case I lost them. I considered putting the candy in my pocket, but if I did that, I would be in trouble if the police stopped me and searched me. In the end, I figured that the safest thing to do was to carry the tiny packet of candies in my hand. That way, if the police did stop me suddenly, I might be able to throw the candy away quickly. I was terrified walking along the street back to my guesthouse. I was relieved to get back to the guesthouse without any trouble, and as I approached Fon's room I looked around carefully to see if anybody was following me. Fortunately, there was nobody around.

Fon and I quickly smoked three candies each. Fon wanted to hide the other four candies in the room and go out, but I didn't like the idea of leaving candy in the room.

"I bought the candy in the middle of a bar," I said to Fon. "What if somebody followed me back to the room? I don't want to leave candy here. Let's just smoke it and then melt the gun like we always do."

"If police want to catch you, they take your blood for test. They no care about candy in your room or not," Fon said.

"Maybe, but I still don't want to leave candy here. Let's just smoke it."

"Okay. Then I smoke my two candy in the shower."

Fon spent twenty minutes in the shower. I smoked two candies during that time, and when Fon came out of the bathroom she said that she had smoked her two candies too, but I was sure that she had just hidden them somewhere.

By the time we left the guesthouse it was a little after midnight. I felt great. I had rested and rehydrated for five days, so now I was feeling the full benefits of smoking candy. I felt happy, full of life, positive, outgoing and I was happy to be with Fon again. I wanted to drink beer and meet new people and have fun. This was the feeling that had hooked me on candy in the first place.

First, Fon and I went to an Irish bar behind our guesthouse. The bar was full of people when we arrived but all the lights were off. It was still early so I thought there must have been a power cut. I asked the owner if we could order drinks.

"Sorry mate," he said. "The local security asked me to close early tonight. They gave me a ten-minute warning about fifteen minutes ago, so everybody has to leave."

The owner was a young Irish guy. He was very friendly to everybody, but I could see that he was getting annoyed that the dozens of falangs in the bar wouldn't leave. Fon and I saw two Lao soldiers with machine guns standing on the road outside the bar.

"Guys, come on! It's all gonna kick off here if everybody doesn't leave quickly," the Irish bar owner yelled out. "Trust me! These Lao guards don't mess around."

Fon and I didn't want to stick around in case something kicked off, so we headed towards the bars by the river. We went to a quiet bar with outdoor seating in the back because Fon wanted to sit down for a while. We ordered two beers and sat in silence. There were three falangs sitting across from us – a guy and two girls. From listening to their conversation,

137

I could tell that the guy had been living in Vang Vieng for a while, whereas the girls had only arrived in Vang Vieng that day. They were tired from their journey so they left after they finished their beers. The guy asked if he could sit with us. Fon was completely disinterested in him. She greeted him as he sat down with us, but then she started looking at her phone. He was an American guy in his early thirties. He was wearing a tank top to show off the dozens of tattoos that he had along his arms. He had long black hair and groomed facial hair. This guy could talk the days away. At first I thought he was just a confident, outgoing guy, but then it occurred to me that he was probably on candy. He was telling me that he had been living in Vang Vieng for several months and that he had gone tubing for the seventy-sixth day in a row that day.

"Why?" I asked. "Doesn't it get boring?"

"No, there are new people there every day. It's not my first time tubing, but it's their first time, so it's always cool."

"So you rent a tube everyday like the other falangs?"

"No, I bought my own. I just pay for a tuk-tuk up river to the starting point. But all the tuk-tuk drivers know me by now so I just pay a dollar each time. Sometimes I go tubing two or three times a day. I tube to the end point and then get a tuk-tuk back to the start again. See, I do promotions for some of the bars. We have a deal. If I bring some falangs to the bar, they give me free beer and food. It's not much, but I don't need much. Vang Vieng is so cheap if you know where to stay and where to eat. My room is only two dollars a night."

There seemed to be a lot of falang staying in Vang Vieng for long periods. And why wouldn't they? It's a party town. Cheap accommodation. Cheap food. Beautiful scenery. Hundreds of new tourists pour into the town every day. Lao women in search of falang boyfriends. Drugs. You would only need two dollars a day for a room and five dollars at the most for food. You could get a large Beer Lao for a dollar or two, so basically you could have a fun life for little more than ten dollars a day.

Fon and I moved on to another bar when we finished our drinks, leaving the American guy on his own. I'm sure he found someone else to talk to. We ended up crossing the old suspension bridge that I had been on earlier when I gave Neung a call. Fon seemed to know the area well, so even though it was pitch dark and there weren't any lights along the way, Fon was able to lead the way without hesitation. She brought me to a crowded area in which three bars surrounded a large bonfire. We were in the middle of a river island, with dirt and flattened grass below our sandals. About a hundred falangs filled the space between the three bars. I couldn't see many Lao people. The music was low and the atmosphere was very chilled. I didn't really like that hippy, backpacker vibe. I went to get a couple of beers at one of the bars, and when I came back Fon was talking to a young, blonde haired falang.

"This is Henry," Fon said. "He live in Vang Vieng long time. He has beautiful girlfriend from England."

I had heard about Henry from several people in Vientiane, including Keith.

"I heard about you" I said. "You are the American guy who is fluent in Lao. My mate, Keith, told me that you plan to open up Lao classes for foreigners."

Keith had also told me that Henry and his English girlfriend wanted to go back home a long time ago, but they had spent all their money on candy and other drugs. Apparently they couldn't ask their parents for any more money, so they were just working in a bar in Vang Vieng for a few dollars a day to get by.

"No, no. Keith is wrong on that," he laughed. "I've no intention of opening any classes. I will go home next month. Actually, I met you before, a couple of months ago, but your hair was really different then."

"I don't' think we met," I said, confused.

"Sure we did. You were with Fon a few months ago in Vang Vieng, right?"

"A few months ago? Well, Fon and I came here in March. Is that what you mean? That's about four months ago."

"I thought it was much more recent than that. Two months at the most," Henry said, also a little confused.

"I was back home in Ireland two months ago."

We dropped the subject and Henry went looking for his girlfriend. Fon and I sat on one of the old tree trunks that were placed around the bonfire. I asked myself whether my hair style had been really different back in March. Maybe it was a little bit longer or a little bit shorter at that time. I couldn't remember.

I looked up at the sky and I was taken aback by how bright the stars were shining. No matter where I had travelled before, the stars had always looked so faint and far away, but in Vang Vieng they seemed to hang low in the sky. The nearest city was Vientiane, but nobody could call that a big city, and it certainly wasn't lit up brightly at night, so there wasn't any big city within hundreds of miles to take away from the beautiful light of these stars. I looked around the sky to find some patterns in the stars, but I didn't really know what to look for.

A falang guy sat alongside Fon and started talking with us. He explained to me that he had met Fon a long time ago in Vang Vieng. He started speaking with her in Lao. I thought nothing of it at the time, and while they were talking I sent Keith a message. He replied straight away, telling me to join him in Dragon Bar. I was ready to leave at this point because I thought sitting around a bonfire talking to other falangs was a bit boring, but Fon and the falang guy were chatting. The falang guy was talking a lot, whereas Fon was just giving one word answers the whole time. She looked a bit bored too. I started to listen carefully but I couldn't understand what the falang was saying. He sounded fluent in Lao. A lot of falangs in Vang Vieng seemed to be good at Lao. Suddenly he turned to me and said, "Sorry, man. I don't mean to be rude by speaking in Lao. We are just chatting about some people we both know."

"Yeah, no problem, man. Work away," I said.

The way he apologized gave me the creeps. I wasn't getting a good vibe from him. I told Fon that I had arranged to meet Keith in Dragon Bar, so we brought our beer with us and left the falang by the bonfire. As we approached the old suspension bridge to get back onto the mainland, a falang guy was walking past me, and when he saw Fon, he nodded at me and said, "I like prostitutes too, mate."

I wasn't too happy with his remark.

"She's not a prostitute. I've been living in Laos for over a year and she has been my girlfriend for a long time."

"Oh shit. Sorry, man. I didn't mean anything by it. My bad," he said, and he appeared genuinely sorry so I left it at that.

A few minutes later Fon and I couldn't find Dragon Bar so I asked a falang for directions. This guy's response pissed me off. Instead of just giving me directions he said, "It's down that way, but I don't think they serve prostitutes."

I explained that she wasn't a prostitute and that we were in a long-term relationship, but this falang was drunk so he probably didn't even understand my explanation.

He just mumbled, "Sure, sure. Take your prostitute to the bar."

I started roaring at the guy in the middle of the street. Fon was trying to push me along, but I was raging. His two mates were waiting for a sandwich next to one of the nearby sandwich stalls, and when they heard the shouting, they came rushing over. They knew that their friend was drunk and that he was likely to be the cause of the trouble, so they apologized for him repeatedly as they pushed him down the street. Vang Vieng was starting to irritate me. This shit didn't happen in Vientiane.

When Fon and I arrived at Dragon Bar, we still had our beers from the last bar. The bars along the river are all open air so they don't try to keep a track on who bought drinks from where. Keith was standing by the DJ box, talking with a Lao guy. He rushed over to me and Fon as soon as he saw us. Fon went to the bathroom.

"He's gonna let me DJ later. You should stick around," Keith said.

"We'll be off soon, mate. Sorry. We'll probably smoke back in the room. You wanna join us later?"

"No, I'm alright. I'll hang around here for a while and then I'll try to get some sleep tonight. I'm wrecked. Haven't slept in three days. Spent about 400,000 kip on candy today. But fuck it. Let's go tubing tomorrow. Fon too if she's up for it."

"Tubing? Fuck, I don't know, man. I didn't plan on going tubing. I don't want to be surrounded by backpackers all day."

"Come on. It'll be a laugh. You must try it at least once while you are here."

"I tried it before."

"Then try it again. We can smoke tomorrow before we go. I heard about one o'clock is a good time to start. I'll try to come to your room at twelve."

"Okay. Fuck it. Let's do it. I'd only be stuck in the room all day otherwise. I'll ask Fon about it later."

Keith went back to his Lao friend, and Fon and I went back to our room. We wanted to smoke candy but we didn't want to go outside to buy it. We had seen armed soldiers earlier in the night so we didn't want to be walking around with candy in our pockets. Fon got the number of a guy from Neung, and after a quick call Fon said to me, "I go get now. You wait here."

I didn't want Fon to go by herself. If I let her go alone, she might leave me waiting in her room for hours. I insisted on joining her. Fon drove

143

to the huge, empty paved area behind the main street in Vang Vieng. Somebody once told me that this huge concrete area was used as an airstrip during the Vietnam War when America carried out an extensive bombing campaign in Laos to disrupt the Ho Chi Minh Trail. Fon stopped her car in the middle of the old airstrip and we waited there for nearly ten minutes. We were in the middle of a huge open space in the middle of the town, in a bright green car. I can't begin to describe how unusual it was for a young Lao woman to own a car. The only other person that I knew who owned a car was the ladyboy from Samlo bar, and that car was a heap of shit. Fon's car was only a couple of years old and in beautiful condition. We stood out like sore thumbs wherever we went, which made doing a discreet drug deal all the more difficult.

A man on a scooter pulled up alongside the car and knocked on the window on Fon's side. I paid 350,000 kip for ten candies. The deal was done in a couple of seconds and we were back at our guesthouse within a few minutes. Fon and I smoked in silence for about an hour and then she went for a shower. I took this chance to look through her bags. She had brought a small backpack full of clothes as well as a handbag with her to Vang Vieng. I was hoping to find something that would give me some insight into what she was doing for the last five days while I was resting in Vang Vieng. First, I looked through her handbag. I opened every little plastic container and every little purse she had. Fon always carried at least three small purses or coin bags and several other small containers in her handbag. Sometimes she would hide candy, boats or receipts in these small containers and purses. I found a matchbox at the bottom of her bag, and when I opened it up I wasn't surprised to see two candies inside. In one of the side pockets I found a scrap of paper with a phone number written on it. I saved the number in my phone under the name 'Scrap'. Next, I looked through her clothes. I pulled out a piece of paper from one of her jeans pockets. It was a Western Union receipt that showed that she had received five hundred US dollars from her 'friend' in France the previous day. The French guy's full name and number were on the receipt. I took out an old scrap of paper from my wallet and wrote them down. I hoped that I would never need to use this information, but it was good to have just in case the worst came to the worst. I placed the Western Union receipt on top of her clothes and closed the bag. I wasn't sure how to feel about another man sending Fon money. It didn't make me jealous or angry because the other man in question was on the other side of the world, and I knew that my relationship with Fon would be over in five weeks. To be honest, I was relieved that she had money because my money was running out quickly.

When Fon came out of the shower, she opened her bag to find fresh clothes to wear. She paused for a split second when she saw the Western Union receipt on top of her clothes. She put on one of her new T-shirts.

"So you looked through my bags," she finally said, as she sat at the edge of the bed and started making a boat.

"You look through my stuff all the time," I said, lying on the far side of the bed.

Fon didn't reply. She started smoking.

"So he sent you money?" I asked, but there wasn't any reply. I tried again, "I don't understand. Why would he send you money? And why would he send you five hundred dollars? That's a lot of money. How often does he send you money anyway? You know I don't have much money left. Have you been getting money from him every month?"

"Not every month. Once or twice a year."

"Why does he send it to you?"

"He want to help me."

"Was he your boyfriend before?"

"No. He know me when I was engaged. We just friends. I help him before when he come to Laos."

"When you were engaged to the English guy? The guy who bought you the car?"

"Yes. The France man know I depressed when engagement was broken. He feel so sad for me, so now he help me sometime. He know that my life ruined after engagement broken."

"Why ruined?" I asked, annoyed that she was being so dramatic.

"I engaged to falang man before. He meet my family. My family show him to all the neighbors. We all so happy then. But then engagement broke and my life bad again. Everyone know I go with English man, so when it finish you think Lao man want me? No, of course not. Lao man never want to marry me now because I with falang before. So, I start come to falang town to find new falang boyfriend. But many falang very bad. They want fuck many women. They no want to take care of woman and marry. They just come want to fuck and go back their country. But France man different. He know I nice person before. He know my life very bad now so

146

he want to help me. But he never come here, don't worry. I no want him to see me like this. I nice person last time he come Laos, but now I not nice."

I had no idea whether Fon was being genuine or not. Her sad story didn't make me feel anything because I had heard that type of story dozens of times before from women in Laos and Thailand.

Fon and I stayed in the room together for the rest of the night without saying a word to each other. I could have gone to my room at any time, but I guess I didn't want to be alone. I lay on the bed and listened to music for most of the night, while Fon fidgeted with this and that. She could spend hours and hours rearranging things in her bag, making boats, adjusting the water level in the gun slightly to make it quieter, and dozens of other stupid little things like that. Finally, the morning came and Fon lay next to me on the bed.

"Keith will come at twelve o'clock," I told Fon. "We will go tubing. Do you want to come with us?"

"Let's see," Fon replied. "I need to rest first."

7

Keith gave me a call at twelve o' clock to say that he would pick me up at one. He said that he didn't need to smoke candy in my room.

"Keith will come at one," I told Fon. "We should get ready."

"I need sleep," Fon replied, lying on the bed with her eyes closed. "You go with your friend."

I didn't like the idea of leaving Fon on her own. I was worried that she might invite someone over while I was away. But I knew that it would be a waste of time staying in bed all day watching her sleep. Before Keith came, I smoked my last two candies and had a quick shower. I still felt good. It had only been twenty-four hours since I last slept, which is not a long time on a candy session.

Keith parked his scooter alongside Fon's car and we walked to the tube rental store. On the way I asked him, "Why didn't you want to smoke?"

"I smoked a couple in my room," he answered, "and I'll smoke another few along the river."

"Do you have some on you?"

"No, but we can buy some at one of the bars. It will be expensive, but hopefully I will meet somebody I know who can help me get them cheaper, like the guy Jack from last night. He said he will be along the river today. If not, then you can impress them with your Lao and ask for a discount."

"I'm not sure if that will do much good. It will be expensive to buy candy along the river if we don't know anyone. That's why I smoked two before I came out. What did you do last night?"

"I just went back to my room and tried to sleep for a while. I left my room at about ten this morning and drove around the place for a couple of hours. Once you go outside the town, the place is fucking beautiful, man."

It only took a couple of minutes to walk to the store, but it was a difficult walk because the sun was blazing down on us. I had to cover my face with both hands.

"When we are tubing, I'll need to stay in the shade as much as possible," I told Keith. "I'm dying here."

When we arrived at the store, there were hundreds of tubes stacked up inside and outside. There were half a dozen falangs standing outside the store with their huge black tubes. Keith and I paid the five-dollar rental fee and signed a document that meant in the case of an accident we wouldn't be able to sue the company. We also had to read a safety manual. The woman said that a lot of falangs get hurt because they are careless and drunk on the river.

"Don't drink too much," the woman started. "Be careful swings and slides. No drugs. And last, try to finish the course before it get dark. It get dark very quick on the river. And end of course the river get shallow suddenly so many falang cut their leg on the rocks. Be careful this one. Tuk-Tuk come in five minutes. Wait here please."

Keith and I waited with the other falangs.

"What swing and slide?" I asked Keith.

"I thought you said you went tubing before?"

"I did, about five years ago, but there weren't any slides or swings then. How can there be a slide on the river?"

"Wait and see," Keith said, amused by my innocence.

Eight of us sat in the back of the tuk-tuk while the driver tied the eight black circular tubes to the roof. He drove us fifteen minutes up the river. The last time I had been tubing was when I was a twenty-year-old backpacker. It was my first time in Vang Vieng. I got the bus from Luang Prabang, and during my first day in Vang Vieng I walked around a bit and I spent most of the evening watching 'Friends'. On my second day I wanted to go tubing, but tubing wasn't something I wanted to do alone. As I was walking around the town aimlessly, I saw a guy named Ben in one of the 'Friends' restaurants. I had met him the previous day on the bus from Luang Prabang, so I asked him if he would like to go tubing with me. Ben was traveling alone too so he seemed delighted to have someone to hang out with. We rented tubes, got a tuk-tuk up the river and started tubing. Back then tubing was not very popular. As we floated down the river there was complete silence most of the time, and we only saw a couple of other falangs tubing that day. The scenery was beautiful along the Nam Song River. Except for a few bars, we couldn't see any man-made structures for miles. The water was brown and the beautiful karsts of Vang Vieng towered above the leafy trees and bushes that lined the river. There were about four bars along the river back then. The bar staff would hold huge sticks out into the middle of the river for the falang to grab onto, and then the bar staff would pull you in calmly and slowly. Ben and I stopped at one bar. It was a nice, simple bar with dark wooden tables and chairs and a thatched roof. We were the only customers in the bar. It was very peaceful. We stayed in the bar for an hour and chatted over a couple of beers. Then we jumped back onto our tubes again. When we were coming towards the end of the course, I found myself about a hundred meters ahead of Ben. All along the river there were tree branches hanging over the river bank. I wanted to slow myself down so that Ben could catch up with me. I reached up and grabbed one of the branches, but when I grabbed it I heard a sudden eruption of a buzzing noise. Bees! I could suddenly feel them buzzing around my head. I must have disturbed a bee hive. I was terrified of being stung to death, so I used my hands to paddle down river as quickly as I could, leaving Ben far behind. I was prepared to jump into the river at any moment to get away from the bees, but fortunately they didn't follow me. When the water became very shallow, I walked to the side of the river and waited for Ben. He arrived a few minutes later and we went for lunch in town. It was a nice day, a nice memory. But from the backpackers that I had spoken to in Vientiane over the past year, I knew that the tubing scene had changed a lot since then.

From the back of the tuk-tuk I heard dance music coming from up ahead. Keith looked at me and he asked, "You ready?"

We got off the tuk-tuk and waited for the driver to untie and unload our tubes. We were in the middle of nowhere. All I could see were green fields spread out to my right and a line of green trees to my left. When the tuk-tuk drove away, the starting point of the tubing course was

151

revealed to us. There were about fifty falangs standing on a wooden platform alongside the river. Some of them were moving erratically to the dance music that was screeching through the air. I could tell that the speakers were not made to be that loud. The sound was too sharp and it was giving me a headache. I could see a lot of Beer Lao among the falangs. Everbody seemed to be having a lot of fun. For a lot of them, tubing was their sole reason for coming to Laos so they were determined to make the most of it.

"What do you think?" Keith asked me. "You wanna have a beer here?"

At that very moment, a young lad with 'Vang Vieng 2010' painted on his back in fluorescent paint yelled, "Legend!" at the top of his voice and jumped into the river.

"Let's get a beer in the next place," I said.

There was a small, steep incline down to the river, so it was difficult for us to maneuver our bodies onto our tubes. I nearly fell into the water at one point but I managed to get my ass onto the tube in the end. Immediately to our left there was a long rope that allowed people to fly through the air and fall into the middle of the river. As soon as Keith and I got on our tubes, a young lad jumped onto the rope but he couldn't get a hold of it properly so he fell straight down onto dry land. Keith and I looked back to see if he was alright. We saw his friends rush to his side and fortunately the young lad got to his feet quickly.

The river had changed a lot since I had last seen it. The last time I went tubing, the river was brown but on this occasion the water was clear.

It must have been because of the time of the year. But the biggest change was the amount of bars along the river. There seemed to be dozens of large open-air bars, each filled with young falangs dancing and drinking beer. It was weird to see this kind of party scene on a river in rural Laos.

"Let's try this bar up here, mate," Keith said. "Jack said he works there sometimes."

There were about thirty people in the open-air bar. Keith and I ordered a beer each. The staff served us the beer and a shot of whiskey each.

"We didn't order whiskey," I said.

"You order beer, you get free whiskey as much you want," the lady behind the bar answered.

That sounds like a great deal, but it was very cheap Lao whiskey. I once visited That Luang (the most sacred monument in Laos) with an American guy who was on a visa run from Thailand. There was some kind of festival going on outside the That Luang complex at the time. One of the stalls was selling Lao whiskey. There were two beautiful women dressed in Lao whiskey branded uniforms. Everything looked very professional and the whiskey looked like a premium product. There was a row of shots of this whiskey lined up at the front of the stall. The American guy was curious about this whiskey so he asked, "How much for one?"

"30,000 kip," one of the ladies said.

The American guy handed the girl 30,000 kip (three dollars) and downed a shot of whiskey in one go. Then one of the ladies handed him a bottle of the whiskey. Both of us were shocked. We thought it was 30,000 for a shot, but it was actually 30,000 kip for a full 700 ml bottle, and the shots were free samples.

I had tried Lao whiskey a couple of times in Vientiane but it almost ripped the stomach out of me. I didn't want to try it again, especially not on an empty stomach.

This bar was much quieter and more laid-back than the first bar. Alongside the bar there was an area with a sign that read 'Mud Fights'. The ground didn't look wet enough for a mud fight that day. I guess mud fights were only held there during the rainy season. A tall, cheerful American guy came up to us and said, "Guys, free whiskey. Let's do a shot each."

"No, mate. We're alright," I said. "Do you work here?"

"Kind of. I hang out here during the day. I mingle, hand out some drinks, and in return I get free beer and they feed me too."

"Do they have a 'special' menu here?" Keith asked.

"Yeah, sure," the cheerful falang replied. "I'll get it for you."

The falang brought Keith the 'special' menu, drank a shot of whiskey in front of us and then carried on mingling with the other falangs. Keith looked through the 'special' menu carefully.

"I can't see candy on the menu," Keith said, agitated.

"Why don't you try something else?" I asked.

"Like what? Magic mushrooms?"

"No, don't try that shit," I said. "I tried mushrooms a few years back in Vang Vieng and they did fuck all. I paid about 20 dollars for a big box. I brought them back to my room and ate them. I stayed in my room all day waiting for the affect to kick in but fuck all happened. It's a scam! How

154

about opium?"

"No, I don't want to try anything else. I've already taken candy and valium today. Better not add anything else into the mix."

"You mean you took valium last night so you could get some sleep?"

"No, I couldn't really sleep. I just rested in my room. In the morning, I smoked a few candies, and then before I came to meet you I took a couple of valium to calm down a bit."

"And now you want to take candy? That's crazy man. You should be careful with that shit. Candy brings you up, then valium brings you down, and then candy brings you back up again. And then you drink beer in between too. That's gotta be dangerous."

"I know. Last week I took candy, valium and viagra in the space of a couple of hours. I started getting dizzy while I was taking a shower so I had to lie down on the bathroom floor for nearly an hour. Sarah was asleep in the room. Fuck knows what she would have thought if she had seen me."

Keith called over the bar staff and asked her quietly about candy.

"Yes, we have. 100,000 kip." she said.

"Wow! That is so expensive. I can buy it in Vientiane for 25,000," Keith said.

"This no Vientiane."

"I know, but 100,000 is too much. I am friends with Jack. He is a Lao man. He says he works in this bar sometimes."

"Yes, I know Jack. Okay, then I can give you for 70,000."

Keith told the lady that he needed to think about it for a few minutes.

"That's expensive. Let's ask in another bar," I suggested.

"Will you smoke too?" Keith asked me.

"I smoked two right before I met you so I don't really need to smoke right now. Plus, I only have about 200,000 kip on me. But I guess I'll smoke one."

"Talk to her in Lao and try to get the price down to 150,000 for three. She probably thinks we are normal falang. If she knows that we live here, I'm sure she will give us a better price."

That's the way things worked in Laos. I couldn't disagree with him. We spoke with the lady behind the bar again. I spoke with her in Lao and eventually she agreed to sell us three candies for 150,000, as long as we agreed not to tell other falangs about this price. We agreed. The lady handed us a white plastic bag with a gun and a cigarette box inside. There was a lighter and some boats inside the cigarette box.

"You smoke in toilet, but quickly," the lady told us.

Keith went first. I stayed by the bar and drank my beer. I noticed two young Lao women sitting at a table with two falangs. I thought I recognized one of the women from Samlo. When Keith came back, I pointed out the woman to him.

"Doesn't she hang out in Samlo and Don Chan?" I asked him.

"Oh, shit! Yeah, that's Nok. I fucked her a long time ago. That's her mate, Dee."

I took the white plastic bag from Keith and I headed to the toilet. The toilet was just an old wooden structure behind the bar. Grass was growing through the wooden floor and there were wide gaps between the planks in the door and walls. People could easily peep through any one of these gaps and see what I was up to. For this reason, I smoked the candy as quickly as I could. As soon as I started smoking, I heard a knock on the door. I nearly shat myself.

"Who is it?" I asked, as I hid the gun behind the toilet.

I was ready to throw the boat down the toilet, but then I heard a woman's voice say, "It's me, Nok. Keith said I can come smoke with you."

"Okay, one minute."

I took one more smoke from the candy and then I opened the door for Nok.

"Sorry," she said, very sweetly. "Is it okay if I smoke a little? Only a little, I promise."

"Sure. You can have the rest of this. There's about half left," I said, handing her the boat and gun.

When I went back to the bar, Keith apologized to me.

"Sorry about Nok, man. She came to the bar to buy a beer. She asked about the plastic bag. She knew that we were smoking so she asked if it would be alright to interrupt you. She said she will return the favor when she gets back to Vientiane."

"No, it's alright. I didn't need to smoke anyway. I gave her about half of it and she was really nice about it too."

"Nok is cool. She gave me her number," Keith said, grinning brightly. "She will come over to my place tonight."

"What about the falang she is with?"

"They will all go out to a bar together and then she will say she is tired and leave early, and on the way back to her room she will drop by my place."

"What about Sarah?" I asked.

"Long story. I'll tell you in the next bar."

We finished our beer and got back on our tubes. Up ahead I could see a huge, blue structure.

"What the fuck is that?" I asked Keith.

"That's the slide we were talking about earlier."

This giant blue concrete tube was placed on grey concrete pillars that rose twenty feet above the water. The tube didn't drop you into the water, rather it threw you into the air and left you fall to the water from twenty feet.

"How the fuck did they manage to build that out here in the middle of nowhere?" I wondered.

"Fuck knows. But they managed it. I don't think it is in use these days though," Keith said.

"What a death trap!"

We stopped in the bar right next to the slide. There were two wooden platforms alongside the river and they were both full of falangs. Again, this area was much quieter and more chilled out than the bar where the tuk-tuk dropped us off. We sat on one of the wooden platforms and drank our beer, like the rest of the crowd. On the other wooden platform there were about a dozen people dancing around, but the music wasn't very loud. Suddenly I got a nosebleed.

158

"Have you been picking your nose again?" Keith joked.

I couldn't help but laugh. I wasn't prone to nose bleeds so I was a little worried about why I suddenly got one. But the beauty about smoking candy is that you don't worry about anything for long.

All the other falangs seemed to be having a great time. They were all mingling with each other, doing drinking games and dancing around the place like it was a huge festival on the river. But Keith and I were detached from all that. We just sat on the wooden platform drinking beer. We had both been staying in Laos and hanging out with Lao people for so long that we found it awkward to mix with falangs.

"Tell me about Sarah anyway," I said. "Are you still with her?"

"Sarah? Yeah, I am still with her. I'll head back to Vientiane in a few days and we will see what happens. I told you that she is still living with her ex-husband, right?"

"Yeah, you mentioned it."

"Well, last week I collected Sarah from her house and we went into falang town for dinner. Her husband must have followed us because when we pulled up outside the restaurant, he suddenly appeared and pushed me off my bike. He dragged Sarah into the car and drove off."

"Fuck, man! That sounds like a weird situation. You are better off out of it, I reckon."

"Nah, it will be alright. Sarah told me to let things cool down for a few days so that's why I decided to come up to Vang Vieng. A few days before that she brought her kid and we all went to the riverside together one day. It was nice. Cute kid."

159

"But doesn't Sarah know that you smoke candy?"

"No, she thinks I don't smoke. She heard from a few of her friends that I smoke, but I told her that I had tried it a few times before but I don't do it anymore."

"And she believes you?"

"Yes. Of course."

"Doesn't she wonder how you can get by with so little sleep, or why you sweat so much or eat so little? Have you ever actually been able to eat a full meal in front of her?"

"That's the biggest problem. She wonders why I don't eat, but I usually say that I ate something right before I met her. Or when we go out at night I say that I can't eat much when I drink beer."

"And you still think she doesn't smoke?"

"Here's the thing, she doesn't sleep much either. She is really skinny, she barely eats anything and most of her friends smoke candy. But I'm pretty sure she doesn't smoke. I mean, she stays in her home for several days at a time, and then I collect her and we stay together for the night, and I bring her back the next day. She doesn't have any chance to smoke."

"So you will keep seeing her? It sounds like the ex-husband might make more problems if you keep seeing each other."

"Sarah said that he wants her back, but she doesn't want it. He offered to build a new house for her mother if they get back together, but Sarah hates him now. She wants to come stay with me, but she can't because of the kid."

"Whatever happens, just be careful. If he finds out that you smoke, he might try to make a problem for you with the police."

Keith nodded his head slowly in agreement.

We slowly floated down the river for about fifteen minutes. I noticed that the bars were getting quieter and quieter as we moved down river. A group of kayakers passed us.

"Did you ever go on one of those kayaking tours?" I shouted over to Keith.

There was about a fifteen-meter gap between our tubes.

"No," he said. "I'd like to one day but I never got around to it."

"How about the caves?"

"No. Never been."

In total, I had stayed in Vang Vieng for about two weeks of my life, but I had only ever walked along the main streets and floated along the river a couple of times. Some tourists came to Vang Vieng to kayak on the river and in the caves, and some tourists even go rock climbing, but I had used my time and money on other things. It was the same with Vientiane. Even though I had stayed in Vientiane for more than a year, I barely knew the city. I only ever walked around the same few streets by the river, and every now and then I would walk as far as the morning market. There aren't any inner-city buses in Vientiane, and of course there isn't any subway. There aren't any taxis either; Instead, there are tuk-tuks, but they rip falangs off. That's why I used to walk everywhere before I met Fon. I thought I would be able to see more of Vientiane with Fon, but we only ever drove from my apartment to Don Chan and back, and once a month we would drive to her parent's home in the outskirts of Vientiane. Keith, on the other hand, had a motorbike, so he would often drive around the city for hours at a time, even in the middle of the night.

"Why the fuck do you smoke candy, which is basically speed, and then lay in bed all the time? It makes no sense to me," he often said.

"Cos my heart is fucked," I used to tell him. "I can literally feel my heart skipping a beat sometimes."

"You're fucking paranoid, man," he would say, just like Ted used to say to me.

We were approaching the bend in the river. There was a bar located on top of a high ridge just before the bend.

"I think this is the last bar before the end," Keith said.

"Then let's stop for one last beer," I suggested.

When we got off our tubes, we had to go up a lot of wooden steps and then climb a rope ladder to get into the bar. The place was completely empty except for one middle-aged Lao man standing in front of us. He welcomed us with a big smile.

"Welcome to my bar. You guys stay and have drink."

We sat down at a table near the back. The roof was very low and the bar was surrounded by bushes so we couldn't see out over the river.

"What the fuck is this place?" Keith asked me.

"It's the last bar before the end of the course," I said. "You'd think there'd be more people."

"I guess people don't know it's the last bar."

We ordered two bottles of Beer Lao with ice, and Keith asked to see the 'special' menu. The man seemed happy that Keith wanted to order from the 'special' menu. There's a lot of profit in drugs when you are charging falangs four times the normal price. Keith haggled with the guy over the price of candy. The menu read 'Yaba – 100,000 kip (smoking tools included).' Keith told the guy about the price of candy in Vientiane and in Vang Vieng town, he talked about how long he had lived in Laos, and he got me to speak in Lao again, all in an attempt to get the price of the candy down. It worked. Keith got the price down to 60,000 kip for one candy. He went to the bathroom in the back to smoke. The bar owner and I spoke in a mixture of broken English and very simple Lao.

"This is the last bar before the end, right?" I asked him.

"Right. Last chance for beer. My bar," the man said proudly.

"Most falangs don't know this is the last bar. They don't know it is their last chance to have a beer on the river before the end. I think a lot of falangs go around the last bend and they are surprised that there isn't another bar before the end."

I had to repeat and simplify my sentences for him, but eventually he understood my point.

"You should make a sign," I said. "Something like 'Last bar before the end! Last chance for beer!'"

The guy disappeared out the back of the bar for a few minutes, and when he came back he had a paint brush, a bucket of white paint and a large square piece of wood in his hand.

"Please, help me," he said, handing me the paintbrush. "You have good idea. You make sign, please."

163

I had nothing better to do while I was waiting for Keith, so I started painting the words onto the wooden sign in large white letters. Keith came out of the bathroom and handed the bar owner money for one more candy.

"What the fuck are you doing?" Keith asked me when he saw me with a paintbrush in my hand.

He rushed back to the bathroom before I had a chance to answer him.

I made the sign using the words that I had originally suggested: 'Last bar before the end! Last chance for beer!' The bar owner didn't even wait for the paint to dry. He took the sign and placed it on the ridge alongside the rope ladder.

"You should make bigger sign if you can," I said to him.

"Yes, I buy big wood and make big sign tonight. Thank you."

The owner stayed next to the sign and waited to see if falangs would take any notice of it. After only a couple of minutes he came back into the bar with a big grin on his face. He welcomed two falang girls into the bar. They ordered a beer each. I ended up talking to those two girls and they asked me to sit with them. They were both from Manchester, England. One of them had long straight black hair and the other girl had long wavy brown hair. They were art students on a two-month backpacking trip around Thailand, Cambodia and Laos.

"I did that very same trip myself after my second year in university," I told them. "It was the best trip of my life. I hope you are having as much fun as I had."

"And where have you been on this trip?" the black-haired girl (the more outgoing and confident of the two) asked me.

"Mainly Laos," I said, a little awkwardly. "I live in Vientiane."

"Working? English teacher?" the brown-haired girl asked.

"No, just hanging out. It's so cheap that I decided not to bother working."

"How long have you been living in Vientiane?"

"I went back home for a few months earlier in the year, but I've been in Vientiane for over a year all in all."

"We just came from Vientiane, but we thought it was so boring," the black-haired girl said.

Falangs who visited Vientiane for a few days were always surprised to hear that I enjoyed living there.

"I know it seems like a kind of boring place to visit for a few days, but it's a really nice place to live," I told them.

"But why did you choose to live in Vientiane?"

I had this exact same conversation dozens of times at the bar or at the pool table in Samlo, and it was always awkward explaining that I initially decided to stay in Vientiane for a month or two to rest and try to write. The next thing I knew, seven months had passed by. Then I met Fon and I got hooked on candy, and then another four months passed by. My return flight was booked for the start of April so I said goodbye to Fon and candy. On the overnight bus from Vientiane to Bangkok I was already thinking about how and when I could come back to Laos. I stayed in contact with Fon and I returned to Laos at the start of June. After a few weeks back in Laos, I knew that I had made a big mistake coming back. Problems with

Fon. Heart problems. Stuck in a shitty apartment all day. Wasting time. Wasting money. Big mistake! I couldn't explain all this to everyone, so whenever someone asked me how I ended up living in Vientiane for so long, I usually just shrugged my shoulders and said, "I don't know. It's just a cool place to live."

A group of six guys came into the bar. They were loud and clearly very drunk. They ordered beer and whiskey. The bar owner looked thrilled. Keith was still in the bathroom. I went to check on him.

"Are you okay in there?" I asked, standing by the bathroom door.

"Yeah, I'm okay. I'm just smoking slowly. I'm done now."

Keith came out of the bathroom and he asked me, "What the fuck is all that noise?"

"Some falangs came. A few of the lads are pissed out of their heads."

Keith and I sat with the two girls. A group of two girls and two boys came to the bar next.

"What's happening here?" Keith asked.

"The bar owner and I made a sign about how it's the last bar on the river, and he hung it outside," I said proudly.

Right at that moment the bar owner came over and placed two candies on the table. Keith and I were shocked. Keith quickly placed his bottle of Beer Lao over the two candies to hide them from view.

"Gift," the bar owner said to me. "You make very good sign. Thank you."

The bar owner and I shook hands. It was nice of the man to show his appreciation, but I felt ashamed that he had given me candy in front of the two girls. They were nice, innocent university students from England. I didn't want them to think that I was some drug addict living in Laos for the cheap drugs. I told Keith that he could have both the candies.

"Are you sure?" Keith asked me.

"Yes, I don't want to smoke. I'm okay with beer."

Keith was baffled.

"I'll ask you one last time. Are you sure that I can have both of these candies?"

"Yes, I'm sure. I don't want to smoke them," I said emphatically.

Keith put the candies in his pocket. He had already smoked two in quick succession in the bathroom. We said goodbye to the two English girls. They said that they would be in the Irish bar at about ten o'clock that night if we wanted to join them.

"Are you sure I can have both of the candies?" Keith asked me again, as we jumped back onto our tubes.

"Fuck no! You can have one, but one of them is mine. I just didn't want to admit to smoking candy in front of the two girls."

As we were going around the bend in the river, it started to get dark. I found myself about fifty meters ahead of Keith.

"Hurry up!" I shouted back at him. "It gets very dark very quickly out here. Be careful."

"You too!" he yelled back, but that's the last thing I heard from him on the river.

A few minutes later I called out his name but I didn't hear anything back. Suddenly it was pitch black on the river. I let the river carry me along and some lights eventually came into view up ahead. I pushed my right hand through the water to steer the tube to the left, towards the lights. I got a fright when my fingertips hit off something hard. God knows what kind of creatures are in that river! But it was only the river bed that my fingers had hit against. The river had suddenly become very shallow so I could stand up and walk the rest of the way. The water barely reached above my ankles. About fifty meters in from the river were the three bars and the bonfire area that I had been to the previous night with Fon. The area was empty except for one young man who was piling hundreds of small pieces of wood for the bonfire. I waited by the side of the river for Keith. After five minutes I started to get worried. I knew that he couldn't have been that far behind me. It occurred to me that I had never even asked him if he could swim. I waited another five minutes, but then the only thing I could do was return to the tube rental store in the hope that he would be there waiting for me. I had heard a lot of bad stories about tubing in Vang Vieng. There were stories going around about falangs breaking their necks on the swings and slides, and a couple of falangs had reportedly drowned in the river after dark. Not to mention other smaller accidents that happened almost on a daily basis.

On my way back to the tube rental store, I passed an old Lao woman at the side of the road. She was sitting on the ground peeling the skin off of garlic cloves and piling them in a basket. We made eye contact for a moment, and then we both looked away. I wondered what she thought of me and the other falangs in Vang Vieng. There I was soaking wet, carrying a huge black tube on my right shoulder. This was probably her hometown – a town that was taken over by the American army in the 1950s and then taken over by tourists fifty years later. Perhaps this woman's family had originally moved to Vang Vieng in the fifties to make money off of the American soldiers. She probably assumed that I was American.

Keith's blue and white sleeveless top was the first thing I noticed when the tube rental store came into view. He was standing among a crowd of a dozen falangs. They were all gathered in front of the tube rental store and looking down at something on the ground. I saw that a man was stretched out on the ground in the middle of the crowd. The first thing that occurred to me was that it was a dead body, but then I saw the head move to one side. Keith stepped out from the crowd when he saw me.

"What the fuck happened?" I asked him.

I looked through the gaps in the crowd and I saw blood pouring from a large gash in the young man's left leg. The blood was flowing down the dirt road in one wide stream, and towards the end the blood split into half a dozen narrow estuaries.

"His leg got ripped open by a sharp rock on the river," Keith said. "He was here when I got here."

"And what happened to you? One minute you were there and the next minute you were gone. I was waiting for you at the end."

"It suddenly got dark and you were way ahead of me. A tuk-tuk driver was shining a light onto the river and he said he would bring me back here for 20,000 kip, so I just went with him."

169

I returned my tube to the store and I got my deposit back. The crowd around the injured guy was getting bigger and bigger as more and more falang returned from the river. Keith wanted to stick around to see what would happen to the injured falang, but I just wanted to go back to my room.

"The bar owner gave you two candies, right? Can you give me my one now?" I asked Keith.

As Keith reached into his pocket to take the candy out, I noticed that his shorts were soaking wet.

"Fuck!" we exclaimed at the same time, when we realized that the water had soaked through the loose plastic and destroyed the candy. Keith's left index finger and thumb were covered in pink from the candy.

"Should I lick it?" he asked me.

"Fuck no!" I said. "Just wash your hands quickly."

I couldn't bear the thought of licking, touching or ingesting candy because I dreaded to think what kind of chemicals they put into it. Yet I had no problem smoking it.

8

When I went back to the guest house, I was annoyed that Fon's car was nowhere to be seen. She had told me that she planned to sleep all day. I knocked on her door but of course there wasn't any answer. I went back to my room and I had a quick shower. I wanted to smoke candy. All I smoked on the river was half a candy in the bathroom in the first bar. I left the door of my room open to keep an eye out for Fon. An hour passed and there was still no sign of her. By now it was almost eight o' clock. I waited for Fon on a bench at the front of the guesthouse. When she eventually arrived, I stood over her as she got out of the car, and I asked, "Where have you been? You said you wanted to sleep all day."

"I went to get my car washed," she said, looking straight through me, her face completely expressionless.

I didn't expect that answer from her.

"How long did it take? I came back over two hours ago," I said.

That was a lie. I had only been back a little over an hour, but I figured that Fon wouldn't know that.

"It took a long time because they were busy. They wash inside car and outside."

So she had been out for at least two hours. I followed Fon to her room.

"Why would you go get your car washed today? Why would you want to get it washed in Vang Vieng? And why in the evening?"

She didn't answer at first, but when we got into her room and we closed the door behind us, she started talking more.

"My car was dirty because I drive from Vientiane on dirty road, and I have money so I should do before I spend it all."

This answer was consistent with Fon's usual way of thinking. If she received a hundred dollars, she would first think about what good and useful things she could buy with the money before she spent it on candy. So, if she had money she would often try to buy CDs, perfume, a speaker, clothes – anything tangible that she could keep for a long time because she knew that the rest of her money would just end up being used on candy. Having her car washed was not exactly the same as buying items in a store and keeping them for years to come, but at least it made sense.

Fon threw a small plastic tube containing ten pieces of candy onto the bed.

"Where did you get them?" I asked.

"From same man last night," she said. "I take a shower."

I looked around the room for a gun. I found a gun and two lighters behind her bed. All I needed now was some tinfoil to make a boat.

"You have any foil for boat?" I asked Fon through the bathroom door.

"My bag is in my car. There is foil in bag, I think. Go and check," she said.

I hid the candy, the gun and the two lighters behind the bed. I

172

took the car keys and the room key with me.

"Let's see how clean this fucking car is?" I said aloud, as I walked across the courtyard towards Fon's car.

According to Fon, the car had been cleaned inside and out only twenty minutes earlier, so of course I expected it to be shining like it had just rolled out of the factory. But as I inspected the outside of the car, it was difficult for me to figure out whether the car had been washed or not. The car wasn't brilliantly clean, nor was it particularly dirty. There were some specks of dirt towards the bottom of the car, but, then again, she had driven the car back to the guesthouse from the carwash centre. I looked closely at the tires. They were dirty. Both the rubber and the allies looked like they had not been washed in a long time. But do carwash centers wash tires? More importantly, do carwash centers in small towns in Laos wash tires? I had never owned or driven a car in my life, so I didn't have a clue about these kinds of things. I ran my index finger along the top of the car roof. It was covered in black dust. Perhaps they had forgotten to clean the roof. I sat in the passenger seat and looked around. I could see that the inside of the car had definitely not been cleaned that day. There was a half-empty bottle of milk in the backseat next to her bag. Did she go meet a guy today while I was out tubing? Did she meet a guy after I left Vientiane? I started to look around for clues.

First, I checked the glove compartment. I found some hair accessories and a couple of CDs – nothing out of the ordinary. I checked all the small compartments by the doors and below the radio. I didn't find anything unusual. If a guy had been in this car with Fon, he obviously would have sat in the front passenger seat. I looked at the floor for footprints. Nothing. I shone a light on the door handle and the window at an angle to see if I could see any handprints. I found one handprint above the glove compartment. The handprint was slightly bigger than my hand. I got a thrill when I found this piece of evidence, but it wasn't exactly conclusive. I went into the back seat. I looked on the floor and I reached my hand into the gaps in the back of the cushioned seat but I didn't find anything. I looked at the milk closely. Fon didn't even like milk, but perhaps Neung bought it. I checked for lipstick. Nothing. But then again Fon and Neung don't really wear lipstick. I checked the expiration date. The expiration date was six days later. I figured that meant that it had been bought very recently. The milk still smelt okay. Next, I checked Fon's bag. It contained all the same things that it contained when I last checked it, except this time I found a scrunched-up receipt at the bottom of the bag. The receipt was from a franchise convenience store in Vientiane. There were only three branches of that franchise in Vientiane. Two of them were in falang town and the third one was only two kilometers outside of falang town. I knew that franchise well because it was the only franchised convenience store in Vientiane. I used to stay near one of them. There were three items on the receipt. The receipt was in Lao, but I could guess that one of the items was the milk because the price matched. The other two items were a dollar each. They could have been anything. The receipt was from two days ago at ten PM. That was enough information for me to put a picture together. Fon didn't like to go to bars in falang town before Don Chan, and she never went to a convenience store for drinks or food in the middle of a candy session. So,

I figured that she arrived in falang town at ten o'clock, bought what she needed in the convenience store (perhaps chewing gum so that she could use the foil to make a boat, and a small beverage so that she could use the bottle to make a gun), and then went to a room in a cheap guesthouse. She probably smoked and put on makeup in her room for a few hours and then went to Don Chan between one and two AM. After Don Chan she would have gone back to her room, smoked some more and then waited in the room until the following evening. Fon always waited for nightfall before she drove from Vientiane to Vang Vieng.

The only thing I couldn't figure out was who Fon had been with. I doubted that she had stayed with only Neung the whole time. I started to wonder about Keith. Was it a coincidence that he had come to Vang Vieng the same day as Fon? Keith rode his bike to Vang Vieng, so I knew that he didn't catch a ride from Fon. But perhaps they had met in Don Chan, smoked candy back in one of their rooms and then decided to go to Vang Vieng the next day. But I stopped myself there. I was only guessing, completely taking swings in the dark. Candy makes people paranoid. I didn't want to be paranoid. The receipt was a tangible piece of evidence that allowed me to make reasonable assumptions about what had happened based on what I knew about Fon. But I didn't have any reason to drag Keith into this.

"I think they forgot to clean the inside of the car," I said to Fon when I went back to her room. "The floor is filthy and they left this bottle of milk in the back seat."

"They didn't forget," Fon replied, sitting at the edge of the bed

175

rubbing cream onto her legs. "I told them leave the milk."

"Since when did you start drinking milk?"

"I need start eating healthy things. Look at my legs," she said. "There little bumps on all my body these days."

I looked closely at her legs. It kind of looked like she had goose bumps on her skin. I started making a boat out of foil that I got from Fon's bag, but Fon pleaded with me, "Please don't smoke here. I need sleep and I need clean air for my skin. If you want smoke, please go your room. You can take the candy. Just leave some for me for drive back to Vientiane. I drive back Vientiane tomorrow night."

"So you will sleep now?" I asked.

"Yes, I need sleep. You take everything to your room. I message you tomorrow when I wake up. You should rest too. You smoke too much."

"I was resting before you came to Vang Vieng," I said, suddenly irritated.

I took the foil, five candies and the two lighters to my room, but I left the gun behind Fon's bed. I didn't want to carry the gun outside, even if my room was only two doors away.

I smoked three candies in quick succession. I sent Keith a message and called him a few times but he didn't get back to me. I had two candies left but I needed to take a break because my heartbeat was off the charts. I lay on my bed in the hope that my heartbeat would slow down a bit. Every time I turned my body from one side to the other it felt like my heart would jump up through my throat. I placed two fingers against my wrist to check my pulse. My heart was skipping a beat nearly every thirty seconds, and every time this happened, I got that terrible feeling in my throat. So, I stopped moving completely and lay perfectly still for a while. In some ways, candy made me feel very at ease. I could stay in the same position for hours.

I kept checking my phone in case Keith called. I didn't want to go outside, nor did I want to be alone. If I was back in Vientiane, I could just call somebody to come to my place. But in Vang Vieng I didn't know anyone except Keith and Fon. I didn't want to be in Vang Vieng anymore. The room was only about a dollar cheaper than in Vientiane, but candy was so much more expensive in Vang Vieng. I came to Vang Vieng to save money, but now that I was smoking candy again it made much more sense for me to head back to Vientiane. I made up my mind to go back to Vientiane the next day, with or without Fon. As far as I could work out, I still had two more nights left in this room, but that wasn't a good reason to stay.

Before midnight I went to an internet café to call my parents. While the phone was ringing, I took a few deep breaths and reminded myself to speak slowly. The last few times I called home, my parents asked me why I was speaking so quickly. I told them that I had been drinking but they knew as well as I did that alcohol doesn't make you talk that quickly. When I went home in April my parents were shocked by how skinny I had become. They must have suspected something. They must have wondered whether it was drugs that had made me so skinny. My mom didn't like the idea of me staying in Laos. Several old men in our town started going over to Thailand after they got divorced or after their wives died. Some of them even brought a young Thai woman back to Ireland and married them. My mom

177

didn't like me going to Thailand because she thought I was only going there to meet women. I tried to explain to her about the huge backpacking scene in Thailand and the beautiful islands in the south, but my mom only associated Thailand with prostitution. She had never even heard of Laos before I went there, so she only associated Laos with Thailand. After a year in Laos I went back to Ireland. My parents thought I would get on with my life, but after a few weeks I told them that I was planning to go back to Laos for the summer. My mom shook her head and sighed in disbelief. I explained to my parents that when I come back to Ireland at the end of the summer I will start looking for a job, so that kept them off my back.

It was nice and comforting to hear my mom's voice. She sounded out of breath when she answered the phone, but she livened up when she realized that it was me.

"Oh, Walt. It's you. It's so good to hear from you. Is everything okay? I was just outside in the garden."

Whenever I called home, we never had much news to share with each other, and my mom never asked how I passed my time in Laos – maybe because she didn't want to imagine what I was up to. During every conversation I have ever had with my mom during my travels, she always said, "If you need any money, just let us know and we can put it into your bank account. There's no need to be stuck. I know you will pay us back. Just let us know."

Usually, I would tell mom that I had enough money and that there was no need to worry, but this time things were a little different. I was running out of money. I still had over a month left before my flight home and there was no way that my money would last until then.

"In the next few weeks I might need to take you up on that offer, mom," I said.

"Just tell me now how much you need and I will lodge the money into your account tomorrow."

"No, it's okay, mom. I have money at the moment. If you send me money now I'm afraid that I will spend it too quickly."

"Okay. Then just let me know when you need it."

My mom asked me one more time about my flight home. She asked me every time I called.

"Me and your dad will be at the airport to pick you up," she always said. "Just let us know the time of arrival and the flight number in case anything goes wrong."

Back in my room I started packing my stuff. I didn't have much things so it didn't take long. I had two candies left. I considered keeping them to smoke right before I checked out and left for Vientiane, but I knew I wouldn't be able to wait that long. I smoked the two candies over the next hour and then I melted the gun and ripped it into two pieces. I put the gun at the bottom of a plastic bag, threw some other rubbish on top and then went outside to dump the bag near the reception desk. Now that I didn't have any candy left, I didn't want to be in a room with a gun. I was always worried that somebody would come to my room and find that kind of stuff. Maybe Fon wanted to make a problem for me. Maybe the owner of the guesthouse heard the bubbling water from the gun and then

179

reported me. Maybe somebody saw me or Fon buying candy outside. That type of thing always played on my mind, especially when I was in a room alone with guns, boats and candy all around me.

When I stepped out of my room, I thought I saw the door of Fon's room close suddenly. I took off my sandals and placed the plastic bag on the ground because they both made some noise when I walked. I approached Fon's door very quietly. I placed my ear to the door, to the line between the door and the doorframe. Since I started smoking candy with Fon, there were several times when I had to listen through a door, and after a while I figured out the best part of the door to place my ear was the gap between the door and the doorframe. In Laos, where they use old wooden doors in the cheap guesthouses, it is far better than placing an empty glass up against the door.

I listened carefully, but all I could hear was the sound of the fan's propellers going round and round. I went down on my hands and knees and I tried to peep through the tiny gap between the door and the tiled floor. I couldn't see anything, but it was clear that the light in the room was off. But then again if Fon had heard me open my door just as she was welcoming a guy into her room, of course she would stay silent and keep the light off for the next few minutes. So, I waited. I waited there for thirty minutes in complete silence. At times I thought I heard whispers from within, but I could never be sure. I put my sandals back on and threw out the rubbish, all the while keeping an eye on Fon's door. The back windows were barred so the front door was the only way anybody could leave the room. I went back to Fon's door and listened carefully again. The sound of the fan was so loud that it could probably drown out the sound of two people whispering if they were standing at the other side of the room or lying on the bed. I heard the sound of a motorbike approaching the guesthouse. At this time of the night the roads were completely empty so the sound of a motor bike caught my attention. I turned to the main road to see who was coming. The motorbike slowed down as it passed the entrance to our guesthouse. There was a Lao woman on the bike. It looked like Neung, but she was too far away for me to be sure. She looked straight at me for a moment and then drove off. *Did Fon ask her to drive by and see if I was waiting outside the door?* I wondered.

I walked past my room to the end of the hall and I hid behind the wall. From there I could keep an eye on Fon's front door without being seen. I waited there for nearly an hour. Nobody came out and nobody drove by. I decided to try to look into Fon's room from the back window. I figured that she would have the window open because it was a hot night. The back of the guesthouse was covered in bushes and weeds. There wasn't any path. Before I took a step into the thick bushes, I hesitated. *What the fuck am I doing? Is it worth it?* I asked myself. But I didn't want to let this opportunity pass. I thought I would be able to look through Fon's window and see her there in the room with a guy. I needed to catch her red-handed so that she couldn't deny it.

It was horrible walking through those bushes and weeds in the middle of the night, in complete darkness. I am terrified of rats, insects and all types of creepy crawlies, so that twenty-meter struggle through the back of the guesthouse was a nightmare for me. The other problem was that I

181

was making a lot of noise as I was making my way through the bushes. Branches were cracking as I planted my feet on the ground, and my body was pushing through thick bushes that had not been disturbed in years. I had to pass two rooms on my way to Fon's room. The lights in both of those rooms were off, but the windows were open. *If somebody catches me in this position I'm in a lot of trouble,* I suddenly realized. I had only thought about Fon. I had not considered what the people in the other rooms would think if they saw me at the back of the guesthouse. They might think I was trying to steal something or peek into their room. The ground I was standing on was lower than the floor in Fon's room, so the window ledge was at shoulder-height. As I expected, the window was open and the curtains were not drawn, but the problem was that it was pitch dark. There wasn't a single ray of light from within the room or from outside the window. I couldn't see anything. I took out my phone and turned on the torch. I pointed the light towards the bed and I could see Fon lying there completely still. I scanned the rest of the room but I didn't see anything unusual. The bathroom door was closed, but that was normal. I coughed a few times. I made a few loud steps in the bushes. I shook the phone light from side to side. But Fon didn't move.

When I went back to the front door of Fon's room, I considered the possibilities of what had just happened. If she had heard me coming out of my room earlier, and if she did have a guy in her room, then she would have been listening closely to see if I was still waiting outside her front door. If she was listening carefully, she would have heard me coming around the back through the bushes, so the guy would probably hide in the bathroom and she would pretend to be asleep when I came to the window. Seeing her in bed alone was not proof of anything. There was still a chance that she had a guy in the room with her.

I sat on the tiled floor next to Fon's front door. Every now and then I leant over to put my ear against the door, but all I heard was the fan. Hours passed like this. I wasn't sleepy or tired, but my body felt hollow – light but stiff. I hadn't drunk anything all night, nor had I been to the toilet. Vang Vieng usually has a nice breeze at night, but it didn't reach Fon's front door, so I sweated a lot in the dead air. I needed to drink water, even if I pissed it out a few minutes later, but I didn't want to move from my spot in case I missed something. I closed my eyes and rested my arms and head on my bent knees for what I thought was only a few minutes. Fon's cough broke the silence. I jumped to my feet and placed my ear against the door. She let out a small cough one more time. I knocked on the door quietly and called out gently, "Fon, are you awake?" but she didn't reply. I knocked a little louder and called out her name again. Still no response. I knocked louder again, but then I saw the owner of the guesthouse arrive and open up the reception area. *I can't stay here*, I thought. I went back to my room and drank a full bottle of water while checking my phone. Nothing from Fon or Keith. I left my door open so that I would be able to hear Fon's door opening or closing. I sat at the edge of my bed and waited. An hour later I got a message from Fon – 'I'm awake. Come my room if you want smoke with me. I go Vientiane in evening. You too?'

9

Keith returned to Vientiane the same day as me and Fon. We arrived late at night, so Keith got us a room in his guesthouse. I was reluctant to check into that guesthouse because it was about four kilometers outside falang town. That was alright for Fon and Keith because they had a car and a motorbike, but I didn't have any way of getting around. The room cost five dollars a night. I could get a room for five dollars in falang town, but this room was more spacious and it had a TV. Fon wanted to stay in our old apartment for my remaining month in Laos, but my money was running low. The apartment cost one hundred and fifty dollars a month, plus I would have to pay a one-hundred-and-fifty-dollar deposit. On top of that, at the end of the month the landlord always overcharged me for electricity. When I used air conditioning a lot, she charged me over one hundred dollars, so the next month I cut down and mostly used just the fan, yet she still charged me over a hundred dollars. How could the electricity bill for a small apartment be that much in Laos? I couldn't argue with her about this because she probably knew that I was up to no good in the room. I didn't want to draw any unwanted attention to myself.

By the time we returned to Vientiane, Fon claimed to only have about fifty dollars of her five hundred dollars left. During her last day in Vang Vieng she bought ten more candies for us, a speaker for her Mp3 player and some T-shirts – one of which was for me. She had been generous with the money. I was surprised.

It was time to sleep. During the drive back to Vientiane, Fon and I had agreed not to smoke candy that night and just sleep. I sat at the edge of the bed in our new room, with my bare feet resting on my backpack. I had to rifle through the bag to find my toiletries and some clean underwear, but I just wanted to sit still for a few minutes. My head felt empty. I couldn't think straight. It had been nearly twelve hours since I drank anything.

"Do they sell water at the reception area?" I asked Fon.

She was arranging her clothes on the ground.

"I don't know. Go check."

"And if they don't? I really need to drink something."

"Go ask."

"Later," I said, as I lay back down on the bed.

Ten minutes later somebody knocked on the door. I jolted upright. Keith was out with Sarah so I couldn't imagine who would come knocking on our door.

"Fuck!" I said out loud. "Who could it be?"

"It's Ting," Fon replied calmly, as she walked to the door.

Ting? That name rang a bell but I couldn't put a name to the face. Then, as Fon unlocked the door, I remembered that Ting was the name of our gay candy dealer. *Fuck! Not this shit again,* I thought.

"Why did you call him?" I yelled at her angrily, outraged that she was going back on an agreement we had made only an hour earlier.

She opened the door so that she wouldn't have to answer me.

185

"Look, Ting brought you water," Fon said to me.

Ting didn't stay long. He just dropped off five candies, a packet of chewing gum, a lighter and a few bottles of water. I wondered if people could order a set menu from him. He always brought the same stuff: candies, small bottles of water for people to make guns with, certain packets of chewing gum that had good foil for making boats, and a lighter. The upgraded set would be a couple of bottles of Beer Lao and a bag of ice, but Fon didn't have time for beer this time.

"Get ready quickly if you want go Don Chan with me. I go in ten minutes," she said.

"Why are you going? We agreed not to go."

"I want to go."

"But we agreed we wouldn't go."

"I want to go. If you want go too, get ready quickly."

"I'm exhausted," I said, completely fed up with this kind of situation.

Fon placed three candies into a tiny plastic pouch and threw it onto the bed.

"You smoke later if you want," she said. "I go into bathroom and smoke now, so smoke no bother you. You sleep."

I hid the candies behind the TV. Fon's bag was open on the bed. I had a quick look through her stuff. I saw the Western Union receipt from the French guy again. I found a discreet side pocket in her bag that I had not noticed before. There was some gum and a lighter in this side pocket, but there was also a small coin purse. When I opened it, I was surprised to see that there was one condom inside the purse and nothing else. Fon and

I didn't use condoms. Perhaps she had this condom in her bag from long before she met me. Perhaps she bought it that day. I had no way of knowing. I stared at this condom for a while, wondering what to do with it. I had an idea. I wrote down the expiry date of the condom in my notebook, and the next thing I wanted to do was make a mark on the condom packet with a coin so that I would be able to identify the condom the next time I had a chance to look through Fon's bag. But Lao money consists only of notes. I searched through my bag desperately in the hope of finding an old coin from my trips to Thailand. Fortunately, I found a coin and I made two small scratches on the front of the blue condom packet, and then I put everything back into the bag just before Fon came out of the bathroom.

"I come back soon," Fon said, as she picked up her bag.

I guessed that the real reason she needed to go outside was to receive a scheduled call from her French sponsor.

"Take the key," I said.

"Why?"

"I want to sleep. Just take the key so that when you come back you can open the door yourself. And please don't bring anyone back here. Please. I just want to sleep. I'm exhausted."

"Okay. Okay. I let you sleep. Don't worry."

I fell asleep without washing or changing my clothes. When I woke up, I couldn't recognize my surroundings. I didn't know what country I was in, let alone the city or guesthouse. More than that, I couldn't remember who I was. I couldn't remember my name or anything about myself. Perhaps this can happen to anybody briefly when they wake from a deep sleep, but the frightening thing was that I couldn't recall any information about myself for a full minute. I sat at the edge of my bed trying to think of my first name. It wouldn't come to me. I looked around the room. I recognized my backpack and my wallet and my phone, but I couldn't link those objects to any memories. Then I started to try to recall my family. I could see my parents and I remembered my mom calling my name at dinnertime, 'Walt'. I breathed a huge sigh of relief, and after that breakthrough everything else clicked into place. Laos. Vientiane. Fon. Candy. A cheap guesthouse far away from falang town. Keith in the next room. Fon going to Don Chan and bringing the room key.

I checked my phone. It was nearly ten o'clock in the morning. Fon had not come back yet. I didn't have any missed calls or messages from her. I was furious. Her phone rang out the first two times I called her, and on the third time I heard the automated message saying that the phone that I was trying to reach had been switched off. I was stuck in the room without any water or food. I was starving. Whenever I woke up after a candy session I made sure to eat as much food as I could because I never knew when I would have an appetite again. I wanted to go outside for food. I thought about leaving the door open and going to the reception area downstairs to ask for a spare key, but then I thought about the three candies hidden behind the TV and the bits and pieces of drug paraphernalia that Fon might have hidden around the room and in her bag. I knocked on the wall between my room and Keith's room, but there wasn't any response. I placed a glass against the wall but I couldn't hear anything. All I could do was wait.

I made a half-assed gun out of the bottle of water that Ting had brought me, and I took some foil from Fon's bag to make a boat. I smoked slowly because I had no idea when Fon would return. A few minutes after I started smoking, I got a message from Fon saying that she was on her way back and asking if I was hungry. I placed the candy to one side and replied to her message. I asked her to bring me fried rice and water. I hid the boat and the gun under the bed. *I should eat first,* I told myself.

Fon entered the room with an expressionless face. She didn't give a shit about anything, and she didn't bring any water or fried rice either.

"Where the fuck were you?" I yelled at her.

She started arranging her clothes on the floor again. No eye contact.

"I play cards with friends," she replied.

"But you said you will come back straight after Don Chan," I continued to yell.

She looked up at me and met my eyes for the first time.

"You said you want to sleep. I no want to wake you so I go play cards with friends."

She twisted my words and she found a way to justify her actions. She was a genius at that.

"I gave you the key so that you could come back, like you said you would, and not wake me. When I woke up I couldn't even go outside to get water or food."

"I no want to wake you," she said, completely focused again on folding her clothes neatly.

"And where the fuck were you anyway? What friends? And why didn't you tell me?"

"I no want to wake you. I go play cards with Guy and some friends you don't know."

I looked through Fon's bag as soon as she went to the bathroom. I didn't need long – just a few seconds to open up the small coin bag and see if the condom was still there. I didn't have time to look through all her bag for new receipts or candies that she might have bought during the night. I went straight for the small coin bag. I got an intense mixture of anger and excitement when I opened the coin bag and saw that it was completely empty. *She must have used the condom,* I thought. Finally I had proof that she was cheating on me. Even though I had cheated on her many times, I still felt horribly betrayed by her, but I also felt relieved that I had not been paranoid the whole time. I even felt proud of myself for outsmarting her. I placed the coin bag back in its original place. I lay down on the bed and considered my next move. I couldn't stay with her anymore. I could ask her to leave. No. She wouldn't leave. She would refuse to go, or she might say that she will leave and then while she is packing her bags we might end smoking candy, she feels tired, she needs to lie down, she needs to smoke more before she goes, we call Ting, she looks like shit so she can't go home to her parents looking like this because they will know that she is doing drugs, she should sleep first, she will go home tomorrow, we have sex, we smoke again, and the cycle continues over and over and

190

everything is forgotten. No. I knew that I would have to be the one to leave. I would have to pack up my stuff and go check into a guesthouse in falang town. *But how will I go to falang town? Fon won't bring me.* I hadn't seen Keith since we arrived from Vang Vieng. There weren't any tuk-tuks in this part of town. I needed to think this through.

I took the boat and the gun out from behind the TV and started smoking again. I reckoned it would be a while before I had a chance to buy food.

"You smoking again?" Fon asked me, when she came out of the bathroom.

"You spent the whole night smoking, I bet," I replied.

"You said you hungry. You should eat first."

"No food. No water."

"Go buy."

"Fon, you know, last night when you were smoking in the bathroom I found a condom in your bag, in a small coin bag."

Fon was sitting on the floor rubbing cream onto her legs. I looked at her closely to see if her hands would change rhythm when she heard me mention the condom, but there wasn't any noticeable change.

"But two minutes ago I checked the coin bag and the condom was gone."

"It's in the car," Fon replied calmly, without a moment's hesitation.

I was taken aback by her response.

"In your car? What are you talking about?"

"I left it in my car. I will go get it later."

"Why would you leave a condom in your car."

"I looking through my bag last night and I leave condom in my car because I no need it. No big reason, just I don't need it so I put in car."

I had planned to tell her that I had made two marks on the condom package and that I had written down the expiry date in my notebook, but now I was glad that I had withheld that information. If she had known those things, she surely would have made up a better lie.

Fon rubbed cream all over her legs and then she picked up her phone. After a few minutes she got a phone call. She spoke on the phone for a few minutes but I couldn't understand a word of what she was saying. I could speak a bit of Lao but I think Fon used Thai or very difficult Lao with her friends when she didn't want me to understand what she was saying.

"Who was that?" I asked.

Fon didn't answer me. She looked very composed as she sat cross-legged on the floor rubbing cream into her arms. Ten minutes later Fon's phone started vibrating on the tiled floor. She cancelled the call. A few minutes later she turned to me and said that she would go downstairs to get the condom from her car. My guess was that she had asked Guy or Ting to bring her a condom. They could easily have left a condom on the roof of her car or behind one of the wheels. The last call that Fon got was probably a signal to say that the drop-off had been made.

I wanted to secretly follow Fon to her car to see how she would handle this situation, but Fon brought the key with her. So, if I was to follow her, I would have to leave the door of our room open. I still had two candies stashed away behind the TV, so that wasn't an option. When Fon came back to the room, she threw a condom onto the bed. Pointing at the condom and looking coldly at me, she said, "There's your condom. Happy now? I don't know why you care so much about condoms. And why do you always look through my things?"

Before I looked at the condom, I sat up in bed and I asked her, "Fon, are you sure that is the same condom that was in your bag last night?"

"Yes, same condom. Look, it's Number One condom, blue and yellow, same as the one in my bag last night."

"But are you sure it is the exact same condom. It's not just a different Number One condom?"

"No, I told you," Fon's voice was getting louder. "Last night condom in my bag, but then I put in my car because I no need condom. Now here it is because you want to see."

I picked up the condom and looked at it closely. Fon looked at me. As I had expected, the condom package was in perfect condition. There weren't any marks. I compared the expiry date on the condom with the expiry date that I had written down in my notebook. *I would make a great detective*, I thought to myself as I carried out this investigation. I was so proud of myself. The expiry dates didn't match.

"Fon, last night when I found the condom in your bag, I made two marks on the condom package and I wrote the expiry date of the condom in my notebook. This new condom doesn't have any marks on the package and the expiry date is different."

"You're crazy," Fon replied, completely unfazed by this evidence.

193

"It's the same condom."

"I know one hundred percent that it's not the same condom. Look, here is the expiry date of the other condom," I said, holding the notebook up to her face and shaking it furiously at her when she refused to look at it.

It was difficult to decide what to do next. I couldn't kick her out because she would just refuse to go. If I tried to physically remove her from the room, she would cause a scene and draw unwanted attention to us. Also, I didn't want to make an enemy out of Fon. I always told myself that if I was ever to leave Fon, I must do it as nice and as gently as possible. I didn't want to end things with Fon badly because I knew that she could cause a lot of trouble for me. It would only take one quick phone call from her, and within a couple of hours the police would come knocking on my door to do a blood or urine test.

It occurred to me that I should just pack up my things and walk out the door – no hard feelings, no arguments. But that wasn't easy either. I was worried that walking along the road looking for a tuk-tuk to falang town with a heavy backpack on my back would push my heart too much. Plus, I didn't want to pay for another guesthouse, I didn't want to go out into the sun, and, also, perhaps I just didn't want to be alone. It's hard to hold a grudge when you smoke candy because it releases dopamine (the happy hormone) in your brain. I didn't dwell on the condom incident but I felt that Fon and I had come to the end of the road. We were dragging each other down. We were destroying each other. I had two more nights paid for in this guesthouse. I decided to take those two days to decide my

194

next move.

Fon and I stayed in the room for the rest of the day. Keith was kind enough to bring us some food from my favorite restaurant, and of course Ting brought us water and candy. Fon didn't go to Don Chan that night. Perhaps she was worried that I wouldn't let her back into the room. By two AM all my candy was gone. I went to the bathroom to brush my teeth, and on my way back to the bed I knelt down alongside Fon to see exactly how many candies she had left.

"Is that all you have left?" I asked, pointing at one full candy that was sitting temptingly in the middle of a beautifully made boat. Fon didn't answer.

I lay in bed but I knew that I wouldn't be able to sleep. Instead, my plan was to pretend to be asleep and see what Fon got up to. I did this sometimes. I lay on my back and opened my left eye ever so slightly. This didn't allow me to see anything clearly, but it allowed me to make out any movement towards the end of the bed, the room door and the bedroom door. I lay like that completely still for a long time. The goal was to lie still for so long that Fon would think that I must be asleep. At least an hour had passed when I heard some movement from the window behind the bed. I had never heard any noise coming from there before. I saw Fon walking towards the window. She looked out for a few seconds and then she leaned over me and looked at me closely. I kept completely still. Even when she was looking straight at me, I didn't shut my slightly opened left eye in case it gave the game away. Fon moved towards the window again and opened it. I heard more strange sounds. *Is she trying to climb out the window?* I thought. The only way for me to see what was happening would have been to move my head or to open my eyes completely. I waited a little while longer, but I couldn't hear Fon and I had lost track of where she was in the room. *Perhaps she climbed out the window,* I thought. I decided to open my eyes to see what was happening. If Fon saw me, I could say that I had just woken up. When I opened my eyes, I felt like I had been paranoid because Fon was sitting on the floor at the end of the bed playing with her phone. I took a quick look at the window behind the bed. Everything was normal. I closed my eyes again and waited patiently. I would usually find it impossible to lay perfectly still in bed with one eye slightly open for hours and hours, but after smoking candy it wasn't a difficult task.

A few minutes later, Fon started moving around a lot. I couldn't see exactly what she was doing, but she had taken the unused blanket from the end of the bed and she was doing something with it near the bathroom door. She moved very quietly, but I could see her trying to hang the blanket off of the bathroom door. Over the next hour or so I could kind of see and hear her open and close the bathroom door very quietly. It was difficult for me to make out whether she was opening and closing the room door also because the bathroom door and the room door were very close together. What is she up to? I kept asking myself. I couldn't contain my curiosity anymore. I opened my eyes and sat up slowly. The room was empty. The bathroom door was closed, but the blanket hung from the top of the bathroom door and reached all the way to the handle of the room door, which was also closed. This was perhaps

196

the weirdest thing Fon had ever done. I lay down on the bed and closed my eyes again. Another hour must have passed before I started to get bored. In that time Fon had opened and closed the bathroom door a few more times, but I didn't hear or see any other significant movements. I got out of bed and knocked on the bathroom door.

"Fon, are you in there?"

"Yes."

Fon opened the bathroom door and when she came out she pulled the blanket down.

"What are you doing?" I asked.

"I smoke in the bathroom."

"Why did you hang the blanket off the bathroom door to the handle of the other door?"

"I didn't want the sound of the gun to wake you. You need sleep."

All sorts of strange thoughts were running through my mind, but almost as a kind of punctuation to these thoughts the question 'Am I being paranoid?' kept popping up. I walked to the window behind the bed to have a look outside. It was already morning. We were on the second floor, and the only thing I could see outside our window were huge tropical trees with long branches and wide green leaves growing out of a swamp. I figured that it must have been those branches that had been hitting against our window in the middle of the night, but it was hard to believe that it had been the wind that had moved them. When I thought about the branches hitting against the window and the blanket

197

covering the front door, I wondered about Keith. *Did he hit the branches against the window from his room next door, as a kind of signal to Fon?* I asked myself. *Did Fon hang the blanket on the doors so that Keith could sneak into the bathroom without being seen?* I couldn't figure out if I was being paranoid or not. I mean, I kind of had some evidence, but it wasn't exactly conclusive. I was terrified about becoming paranoid, so I put these strange ideas and incidents to the back of my mind.

10

After lying still on the bed for most of the night, I was up out of bed now and ready to smoke again. I gave Ting a call. He came. I smoked. A few hours after Ting had been and gone, I had smoked all my candy and I started to think about Fon's condom again. Fon was in the bathroom smoking. I saw her car keys on top of the TV. An idea came to me. I couldn't believe that I hadn't thought of this before. First, I put Fon's car keys into my pocket and then I pressed record on my Mp3 player and carefully placed it under my pillow, making sure the microphone wasn't covered.

"Fon, I'm going out for something to eat," I said, standing next to the bathroom door.

No answer.

"I'll go into falang town to Noi's Restaurant. Do you want anything?"

"Fried rice," Fon replied from the bathroom.

I had no intention of going to get food. I just wanted Fon to think that I would be out for a while. Instead of going for food, I wanted to look around the inside of Fon's car. The night before last she had gone to Don Chan night club with a condom in her bag, and she came back the next morning without a condom. I wanted to find more proof that she had slept with someone, and I believed that I would find it in her car. I searched every inch of the car for about fifteen minutes but I couldn't find anything. I searched the glove compartment, under the seats and every other inch of the car. By now it was the middle of the afternoon and the sun was very strong. I couldn't search the car anymore in this heat. I went back to the room.

"Fon, it's me," I called through the door.

I had to knock on the door a few times before Fon let me in. Fon saw that I had come back empty-handed.

"Where's the food?" she asked. "I thought you go Noi's Restaurant?"

"It's too hot outside," I said. "I walked for a bit, but then I had to turn back."

Fon sat on the floor towards my side of the bed, the opposite side to where she usually sat. I lay down on the bed and took the Mp3 player out from under the pillow. The recording was twenty-one minutes long. I turned the volume up full blast and listened very carefully through my earphones. First, I heard my conversation with Fon about me going to Noi's Restaurant, and then I heard me leaving the room. For the first few minutes I could hear the shower running. The shower stopped and after a few minutes of complete silence I could hear the bathroom door open. I could hear Fon walk around the room for a little bit and then it sounded like she sat on the floor somewhere near the bed. There was silence again for a while. Then I heard a knock on the door. The sound was very faint, but it was definitely a knock. To hear everything just a little bit louder, I pushed both earphones into my ears as far as they would go and held them there with my index fingers. Fon opened the door and said something. I couldn't make out what she said, but it was definitely English. Then I heard a man's voice. Again, I couldn't hear the voice clearly, but there was no doubt that it was a man and he was speaking English. Then I heard them kiss. This was unbelievable! When I came up with this plan, I thought I might catch Fon talking with a guy on the phone or something like that. I didn't expect to actually catch her with a guy in the room. I pulled the earphones out and jumped up on the bed.

"You bitch!" I yelled, standing on the bed, towering over her. "Do you know what this is?"

Fon looked up at me. She was in the process of making a gun out of an orange juice bottle.

"What are you talking about?"

"Do you know what this is?" I yelled, this time even louder.

Fon turned away from me and started burning a hole into the plastic bottle.

"When I left the room earlier, I pressed record on this Mp3 player and left it under the pillow. I just listened to it."

I looked closely at Fon for a reaction. Her face looked different now, but it wasn't clear if she was annoyed because she thought I was crazy or because I had finally caught her.

"When I listened to it, I could clearly hear a guy coming here and kissing you."

"No!" Fon suddenly yelled. "You crazy! Why you do like this?"

"I heard it!" I screamed. "You can't deny it any more, you cunt! You fucking slut! I heard it. I heard you open the fucking door and let a man into our room when I wasn't here. And where is the cunt now?"

It suddenly occurred to me that if I ran downstairs I might be able to catch him. Apart from me and Keith there weren't any other falangs in this guesthouse or this area, so if I saw a falang I could be pretty sure it was the guy Fon had kissed in our room. I ran down to the reception area. I walked along the small road in front of our guesthouse for a few minutes. Our guesthouse was located on a quiet back road about a hundred meters in from the main road. There was a large temple complex across from the guesthouse and a couple of noodle restaurants down the road. The road was completely empty – no cars, no motorbikes, no falangs except me. I hung around the car park for a few minutes, but I didn't see any falangs or anyone who looked suspicious. I hurried back to the room to confront Fon again, but she locked the door and she wouldn't let me in.

"Let me in!" I yelled through the door.

"No!" she yelled back. "You crazy! If I let you in, maybe you hit me. I'm scared."

I kept banging and kicking the door, yelling at Fon to let me in.

"I open for you when you calm down again, when I feel safe," she said.

I stopped banging on the door because I was worried that the guesthouse staff might get involved, or, worse still, that the police might

202

turn up.

"Fon," I started, but before I could continue, I saw something move in the corner of my eye.

I looked towards the end of the hallway and saw a man turn around quickly and disappear around the corner. I didn't see enough of him to tell whether he was a falang or a local. I didn't think much of it at the time.

"Fon," I started again. "Please, let me in. Of course I won't hurt you. Just let me in."

"When you calm more," she said.

I sat down on the floor with my back leaning against the door. I was sweating terribly because there was only hot stale air in the hallway. By looking through the key hole I could see Fon's arms moving and part of her face. With my face so close to the door, I realized that there were gaps between the panels in the door. Most of these gaps were razor-thin but one of the cracks was wide enough to let me see through to the room quite clearly. I could see Fon kneeling alongside her bag. She was folding her clothes and packing everything very neatly. She was wearing a baseball cap and a hoodie. It looked like she was ready to leave at any moment. I had been smoking in the room for the last few days. Anybody could have seen me through this gap in the door. Of course I didn't tell Fon about this gap because I hoped I might catch her doing something.

"Fon, please let me in. I need to drink water," I pleaded.

"Go reception. They give you water."

I couldn't bring myself to leave the scene in case I missed

something. Then, as I was kneeling on the ground looking through the gap in the door, it suddenly occurred to me that the man who had disappeared around the corner at the end of the hall must have been the falang who I had heard on the Mp3 player. He must have come back to see what was happening. Perhaps Fon didn't answer his calls or reply to his messages, so he came back to put his ear to our door and listen to what we were saying. I considered running downstairs to try to catch him, but I decided against it. I figured that he would have been long gone by now. I kicked myself for not chasing after him when I saw him turn around and scamper away. I continued looking through the gap, and after Fon finished packing her stuff I saw her sitting on the edge of the bed looking closely at my Mp3 player. She held the earphones up to her ear and she tried for several minutes to find the recording that had enraged me, but she couldn't figure out how to use the Mp3 player. She threw it to one side and picked up her phone.

I sat in the hallway for nearly two hours. I was severely dehydrated and weak. I was worried that I would collapse at any moment. Then I saw Ting walking towards me.

"What you do, Walt?" he asked, laughing. "You sweating."

I was glad to see Ting because I knew that Fon would now open the door. Both Fon and I bought five candies from Ting separately. I hid my candies behind the TV. Before I smoked I wanted do drink plenty of water and listen to the recording again. While I sat at the edge of the bed listening to the file, Fon and Ting sat on the ground drinking beer and making boats. I told them about the gap in the door. Fon covered it with a towel.

"What you listening to?" Ting asked me.

I explained how I had recorded Fon letting another falang into our room while I was out.

"You crazy!" Ting said, with a sly smile. "Fon no do that. She love you."

I listened to the file from the start, from me leaving the room to the part when the falang and Fon kissed. After that, Fon and the falang talked some more, and then I heard something that completely shocked me. I heard a knock on the door and my voice calling out "Fon, it's me." There was some movement and then Fon opened the door for me. I explained to her why I didn't go to Noi's Restaurant, and then there were some loud muffled sounds right before the recording stopped. I was stunned. He was still in the room when I came back and turned off the Mp3 player. I leaned over the edge of the bed quickly to see if he was under the bed. My backpack was there, but it was in the center, whereas it was usually under my side of the bed. I hurried to the bathroom to see if he might be hiding there. Fon and Ting saw that I was flustered.

"What are you doing?" Ting asked.

I turned to Fon and said, "He was still here, wasn't he? When I came back here, he was in the room, under the bed, wasn't he?" Fon didn't even look at me.

"You smoke too much," Ting said patronizingly. "You need relax."

"That's got nothing to do with it," I said. "I have proof. I recorded it all."

I lay down on the bed and listened to the recording again. I tried to think about everything I did when I came back to the room the first time, and I tried to remember if I had seen anything unusual. I remembered thinking it was strange that Fon sat on the floor by my side of the bed, and I wondered if that might have had something to do with my backpack being pushed into the center. *But when did the falang leave the room?* I asked myself. *Was it when I lay on the bed and closed my eyes while listening to the recording the first time? Probably not. It was probably when I left the room to go looking for him downstairs.*

I sat at the end of the bed and said to Fon in a very reasonable voice, "Can you please leave? Please just go. Just take all your stuff now and go with Ting."

"Where I go?" Fon suddenly yelled. "Where I go? Tell me."

"Go home to your family," I said.

"Look at me. How I go home to family like this. If I go home like this, they know I do drug and they never forgive me. I cannot go home."

"Then go with Ting."

"Ting work. I cannot go with him. But I go. I no stay here. Don't worry. Don't worry."

A few minutes later, Ting gave Fon some money, probably a loan, and left.

I had no fight left in me. I hid my five candies behind the TV and just lay in bed for a few hours. I knew Fon would only leave when she was ready to leave, and she wasn't anywhere near ready yet. That evening Keith knocked on the door. He smoked a couple of candies in our room.

"Sarah and her daughter are in my room next door if you want to come say hello to them," he said.

"Her daughter is in your room?"

"Yeah. The three of us went out for dinner. I'll bring them home in a minute, but we just came back here so that I could get some cash.

"This doesn't seem like a good place to bring a kid," I said.

"It's fine. It's fine."

I went next door to see Sarah and her daughter. The kid was about nine years old. It felt weird seeing a kid in this kind of dodgy guesthouse. I told Keith about the condom and the Mp3 recording.

"You need to get away from her," he said. "I can bring you into falang town on my bike and you can get a room there."

"I feel like shit to be honest. I'm not up to moving to a new guesthouse tonight. I'll decide tomorrow. Maybe I'll fuck off to Vang Vieng again, or maybe Bangkok."

Fon and I stayed up all night. Ting visited us around midnight and again shortly after sunrise. The second time he came, Fon only bought two green candies because she wanted to relax her body and sleep all day. I bought five normal candies but I didn't smoke them right away. In the afternoon I paid for one more night in the guesthouse and then I lay alongside Fon and tried to sleep too. I gave it a couple of hours but I couldn't fall asleep, even though it had been more than sixty hours since I had last slept. I smoked the five candies very slowly throughout the day. I

207

decided to sleep that night and move back to falang town when I woke up the next day. By then Fon would be fully rested and surely she would be ready to go home. I looked forward to enjoying my last month in Vientiane without Fon.

In the evening, after I finished all my candy, I melted my gun and flushed the rolled-up one thousand kip down the toilet. I threw the melted gun, the hacked lighters and other small pieces of rubbish into a black plastic bag. I wanted to clear the room of anything related to candy before I went to bed. Right as I was considering the best way to get rid of the plastic bag, somebody started banging on the door. I was instantly filled with a terrible fear.

"Who is it?" I asked.

There was no answer. I opened the window quickly and threw the bag out of the window into the swamp.

Again, 'Bang! Bang!' on the door, far louder and more aggressive than a normal knock. A Lao man said something through the door. I couldn't understand him but he sounded aggressive. Fon was still asleep.

"Fon, Fon, wake up!" I whispered to her in a panic, shaking her by the shoulders.

"What? What?" she asked, annoyed.

'Bang! Bang! Bang!' on the door again.

"Who is that?" Fon asked, suddenly frightened.

"I don't' know. They said something in Lao. Fuck! What do we do?"

Fon sat up in the bed and she said something to them in Lao. A male voice answered back.

"What's happening?" I asked "What did he say?"

"He said open the door. He said there are people waiting for us downstairs," Fon explained.

She looked terrified.

"What do we do?"

"Don't answer the door," Fon said.

The knocking on the door stopped for a few minutes

"Clean everything up," Fon whispered.

"I did it already," I said.

Fon had told me several times that when the police come to your room they do a blood or urine test there and then, so it wasn't enough to just melt the guns and flush the boats down the toilet.

The banging on the door started again suddenly and this time it seemed even louder. Then we heard Fon's phone vibrating under her pillow. She looked at her phone and said, "I have a lot of missed calls from my mom and my brothers."

I looked out the window. By now it was dark so I couldn't even see the ground. We weren't really high up and there was some water below to break the fall if we decided to jump. 'Bang!' 'Bang!' 'Bang!' on the door. 'Bzzzzz.' 'Bzzzzz.' 'Bzzzzz.' Fon's phone vibrating. It was relentless.

Amidst all the noise and panic, I heard my name being called from the other side of the door.

"Walt!"

It was Keith's voice.

"Keith? What's going on?" I asked, terrified that he would say that

209

the police had come for us.

"Fon's family are downstairs waiting for her," he said.

I turned to Fon. I was not as relieved as I should have been because I still thought I had reason to be very worried.

"You believe him?" Fon asked me, looking at me like I was stupid. "How we know he tell true?"

Fon never trusted Keith. Her phone was still vibrating.

"Is that your mom calling you?"

"Yes."

"So answer it and ask her."

Fon answered the call from her mom. The phone call lasted only a few seconds.

"My whole family downstairs," Fon said. "They want to take us home."

Fon and I packed our things quickly. It never occurred to me to refuse to go with them. The whole family (parents, three brothers, young sister and baby niece) were waiting downstairs in the reception area. There were no raised voices or angry looks when we met them. Fon's eldest brother drove her car home and we went with the rest of the family in the father's minivan.

In the minivan, I asked Fon, "Why did they come?"

"They are worried about us," she said. "Mom just said we must go home and rest."

"How did they know we were staying in that guesthouse?"

"I don't know," Fon replied, and that was one of the very few times

I completely believed her.

11

Fon's family home was about fifteen minutes from falang town by car. Her family lived in a large bungalow alongside a small stream. Half of the house consisted of a wide open living room that is common in Lao houses, but during the day, and even in the evening, most of the family sat in the tiled open area at the front of the house because it was cooler there. Beyond the living room there were five bedrooms and two bathrooms. Fon's parents and ten year old sister stayed in one room. Her oldest brother stayed in one room with his wife and their two year old daughter. Her other two brother's shared one room, while Fon had a room to herself. The fifth bedroom wasn't so much a bedroom but a separate living area for the five female workers that worked in Fon's parents' bar. I never visited their bar, but according to Fon it was a place for local men to visit and drink beer with young women. I never got a straight answer as to whether these women were prostitutes or not. One of the bathrooms was for the workers and the other bathroom was for the family.

Fon's family were always very kind to me. They welcomed me into their home and made me feel at ease. During the first few days I mainly stayed in Fon's room all day. I slept for more than ten hours at a time, and when I woke up I just ate some food, drank a large bottle of coke and then went back to bed. Fon wanted to sleep a lot too, but her mom wouldn't let her. She insisted that Fon wake up early and keep to a normal routine. I was a little ashamed because at best Fon's family thought I was really lazy and at worst they knew that I was sleeping all day because of candy. But I couldn't help it. My body desperately needed sleep. When I was eventually able to stay awake during the day, I started spending more time with Fon's family, especially her little sister and niece. We watched cartoons on TV together and drew pictures in my notebook. One day Fon's little sister, Noy, and her friend led me and Fon across the stream and into a neighbor's backyard. Noy opened the rusty door of an old shed and showed us five cute little puppies inside. They were only a few days old. Noy and her friend visited the puppies every couple of hours. It was school vacation at the time, so Noy was free all day. It looked like she had a really normal, carefree childhood. According to Fon she attended a private school in Vientiane. The family had high hopes for her.

During the day I was usually the only man in the house. Fon's two older brothers worked and her younger brother usually went out to meet his friends during the day. Fon's father was often away for a few days at a time.

"Where does he go?" I asked Fon.

"He cuts down tree and sell wood to China," she said.

"Is it legal?"

"No. It black market, but good money. Many people do."

Fon's mom and dad owned a bar nearby, but I guess somebody ran it for them because neither of them went there much. The five girls who worked in the bar stayed around the home all day. They played with

213

the two children and helped Fon's mom with the housework. In the evening Fon's father or one of her brothers drove them to the bar in the minivan. Sometimes visitors would come to the house in the evening. One evening a friend of Fon's brother's wife visited. She brought small bags of milk with her.

"What are they?" I asked Fon.

"Breast milk," she replied. "She have young baby now but she make too much milk."

"So she gives it to your brother's wife?"

"No, she sells it to my brother. He likes to drink that milk."

"He drinks breast milk?"

"Yes. Why not?"

I was shocked. I had never heard of that kind of thing before.

Another evening a friend of the family who worked in a hospital brought over half a dozen IV drips. Fon's parents and two older brother's lay on the floor as the woman hooked them up to drips.

"Why are they doing that?" I asked Fon. "Are they sick?"

"No," Fon answered. "They just do it sometime. It good for body. You want?"

"No thanks."

That was new to me too.

In the evenings I watched movies on my laptop. They didn't have internet, but I had some DVDs. Fon and I were enjoying those peaceful days and we were getting along very well. We planned to stay in her home for a couple of weeks. I told Fon that I wanted to go into the city to withdraw money so that I could give some money to her parents for all the food I was eating. I also suggested that while I was in the city I might be able to stop off at Talat Sao (the morning market) to buy some DVDs. Fon arranged for her brother to bring me into the city the next day in her car. I think her parents didn't want Fon to leave the house. Her brother dropped me off at Talat Sao and he collected me three hours later. I gave Fon's parents a hundred dollars. The next day Fon's parents went out somewhere. Fon's brothers were at work, so it was just me, Fon, the two kids and the five workers left in the house. I was in Fon's room watching a movie and eating ice-cream, as happy as could be.

Fon knelt down alongside me on the floor. She looked very healthy. Her face had filled out a lot. She looked young and cute.

"Do you want to go falang town?" Fon asked.

I had mixed emotions when I heard Fon's question.

"I thought we were going to stay here for a while longer?" I said.

"We can just stay in a guesthouse for a few nights and then come back here. I can't smoke for long time like before. My parents too angry me now. I must come home again soon."

We headed straight for a cheap guesthouse in falang town. We got a room without an air conditioner or a TV for five dollars a night. It was a depressing room. The ceiling was unusually high and the walls were painted in a horrible mustard color. There was a ceiling fan to keep the air moving, but the window in the room was tiny. Within a few minutes of checking in, Ting was in our room selling us candy. We fell into our usual

215

cycle of smoking candy all day and night, only ever going outside to visit Don Chan for a couple of hours at night. Two days passed like this, and on the third day Fon stepped out of the bathroom with a pregnancy test in her hand and casually dropped the bombshell that she was pregnant. I took a close look at the test.

"Where's the box?" I asked in a panic. "I don't know what these lines mean."

I compared the pictures on the box to the test and confirmed that it was indeed a positive test. Fon sat down on the bed and took a sip of water. She didn't seem worried.

"You're pregnant?" I asked, desperately thinking of how to best respond to this news.

"Yes."

"Since when?"

"I don't know."

"When did you realize you might be pregnant?"

"I don't know. Not long ago."

"But...but....I only ever came inside you once a long time ago, when we were in Vang Vieng back in March."

"Really?" Fon replied, a little surprised.

"Yeah, you know I never come inside you. It only ever happened once. I remember it clearly, and that was almost five months ago. There's no way you can be five months pregnant."

"But we don't use condoms."

"I know, but I didn't come."

"But I am pregnant."

I recalled an argument I had with my female friend back home a long time ago. For some reason the subject of contraceptives came up and I mentioned that it was impossible for a woman to become pregnant from pre-cum. My friend said it was possible and that I was being naïve. After that argument I checked online and found that it was technically possible to fall pregnant from pre-cum but only in very rare cases. I couldn't accept that my pre-cum had gotten Fon pregnant. It was far too improbable. I thought the only way I could be the father would be if Fon was five months pregnant, but that was hard to believe too. Before questioning things too much, I first needed more proof that she was actually pregnant.

"I'm gonna go get another pregnancy test," I told Fon. "If I get another test, will you do it to make sure?"

"Yes."

There was a pharmacy around the corner from the guesthouse. There were three kinds of pregnancy tests in stock. I bought one of each and hurried back to the room. Fon tested positive on all three tests. I wondered if she had some secret way to manipulate the results of the test. I told Fon that I needed to pee, but while I was in the bathroom I looked everywhere to see if I could find anything suspicious. I thought that perhaps she had a pregnant friend and that she had used her pee to get a positive result on the test. I also considered the possibility that a pregnancy test might give a positive result if one was to dip it in something like shampoo or body wash. I was desperately trying to make sense of the situation.

"If it's my baby, then you must be about five months pregnant," I told Fon.

"Maybe."

"What do you mean 'maybe'? Maybe it's my baby or maybe you are five months pregnant?"

"You are the father. Who else can be? But I don't know how long I pregnant."

"When is the last time you had your period?"

"I no remember."

I sat in silence for a few minutes while I tried to think of a time when Fon had complained about being on her period, but I couldn't recall her ever mentioning anything about her periods since I had met her. I looked at Fon closely as she picked up her phone and made a call. She looked so thin. *There's no way she could be nearly five months pregnant*, I thought to myself. But then again even a pregnant woman probably wouldn't put on much weight if she smoked candy every day.

"Who did you call?" I asked Fon.

"Ting."

"Why? Is he coming here?"

"Yes.

"But you can't smoke. You're pregnant."

Fon didn't reply.

The one thing Fon and I agreed on was that she must have an abortion. We agreed that all the candy that we had smoked must have done serious damage to the fetus. The point we couldn't agree on was when she should get the abortion. I strongly insisted that we go as soon

218

as possible - that day or the next day at the latest. I was worried that if she kept smoking she would be putting herself in danger if there were suddenly some complications.

"You are nearly five months pregnant," I said, purposefully mentioning the idea that she was five months pregnant to see if she would react. "It's already very late to get an abortion. If we don't go soon, maybe the doctor will say it's too late."

"I go when I ready," she said.

"And when will that be?"

"I don't know. I no have money."

I wanted to scream at her but I took a deep breath and said calmly, "I'll pay."

No reaction.

"So when will you go?" I asked.

"Soon."

"Do you know where you can get an abortion?"

"I ask friend. I think there is one place near university."

"And how much is it?"

I had already agreed to pay for it so she knew that she could just name any price she wished.

"I don't know. I ask my friend now," she said, as she typed a message on her phone.

"Anyway, it's Laos, so it can't be very expensive. I mean, it couldn't be more than a hundred dollars, otherwise nobody would be able to get it done."

My sole purpose for saying this was so that it might deter Fon from naming some ridiculous price.

"My friend say it's 300 dollars."

"300? Jesus! How could it be that much? That's like three months' salary for most people in Laos."

We sat in silence for a few minutes.

"Anyway, I will withdraw the money from an ATM today," I said, and before Fon could reply Ting knocked on our door.

I pleaded with Fon not to smoke, and after that failed, I pleaded with Ting not to sell candy to her. But in the end I gave up. I even sat alongside her and smoked too. Fon didn't have any money left so she had to ask Ting to give her five candies on the slate. I paid for my five candies in cash.

"Why you no pay for your girlfriend?" Ting asked me.

"Because she's pregnant. I don't want to buy drugs for a pregnant woman."

The next day Fon was still delaying her visit to the clinic and she was still insisting that she would go when she is ready. I couldn't bare waiting because I was terrified that Fon would wait too long or that all the candy would cause some serious problem inside her.

"This is crazy!" I told Fon. "You can't keep smoking while you're pregnant. If you don't stop smoking or if you don't go to the clinic today, I'll call your family and ask them to come get us again."

Fon must have thought I was bluffing. She didn't understand how overwhelmed I was by the whole situation. She kept smoking. I searched through my contacts and found Fon's brother's name, Somphone. He had given me his number when I was staying in the family home.

I was nervous when the phone rang. Fon looked at me, but she must have still thought I was bluffing because her face was expressionless.

"Somphone," I said, when her brother answered, "I'm sorry to bother you, but there's a big problem."

Fon stood up from the bed. Her eyes were bulging, and as she tilted her head to the side, she whispered to me angrily, "No! No!"

"What wrong?" Somphone asked.

"Fon needs your help. Can you come here? We are staying in a guesthouse near the river."

"Is my sister sick?"

"Kind of. Somebody should come quickly."

"I at work now. I call mom. She go there. Tell me name of guesthouse."

As soon as I finished the call, Fon started screaming at me.

"What did you do? What the fuck you do?"

Her eyes were full of rage. I had never seen a person so furious in all my life. Anger had stiffened her body and she was almost shaking.

"You kill me!" she shouted. "Now I dead. If my family find out about this, I am dead. You kill me!"

"I had to call someone," I said.

Fon picked up a lighter and threw it at my head, but I ducked just in time. Then she reached for an empty glass and flung it at me with as much power as she could muster. I ducked again and the glass smashed off the wall. Fon ran to the other side of the room to grab an empty bottle of beer. When I saw what she was running towards, I made a quick escape out the door. I knew she wouldn't follow me out of the room. There was an old Lao woman mopping the hallway. She must have heard the shouting and the glass smashing, but she didn't even look up at me. I didn't want to go back into the room so I sat on a bench outside the guesthouse until Fon's family came.

Thirty minutes later a woman pulled up on a scooter. When she took off her helmet I recognized the woman as Fon's friend, Li. Li was Fon's childhood friend. She worked in an office and she had no interest in falangs or falang town. I stood up from the bench to greet her.

"Fon's mom send me," Li said. "She very worried. She say something wrong with Fon."

"Yes, I called her brother for help."

"What wrong with my friend?"

"I'd rather not say. You should ask Fon," I said.

I told Li our room number. I decided to stay on the bench because I figured Fon wouldn't open the door for Li if I was there. A while later Fon called me. She asked me to go get some fried rice and soup in a restaurant nearby so that we could eat with Li in the room. Fon seemed very calm all of a sudden. We ate with Li, and after she left I asked Fon about what had happened.

"My mom send Li to see how I am. Mom trust Li."

"What did you say to her?"

"I told her Walt worried me because he think I sick. I tell Li that last night and this morning I not feel good, but now everything okay, so no need to worry."

"So what now? You will just keep smoking?"

"Why you call my family? Why you want family to see me like this? That my family. I never make problem your family."

"I'm sorry, but I didn't know what else to do. It scares me to think of you smoking candy when you are pregnant."

I partially regretted dragging her family into this, but on the other hand I felt glad that I had tried something drastic to change the course of these ridiculous events.

"So what now?" I asked.

"We need to clean room. My brother, Philaylack, will come later with Nam (her oldest brother's daughter). We need to throw out gun and everything."

"Why will your brother come?" I asked.

"Because my family worried now," Fon said, as she started collecting all the rubbish on the floor. "They think there big problem now because you call them."

Fon agreed to go to the clinic the next day as long as I didn't make any more problems with her family. Fon called Ting and asked him to go buy fried chicken from a popular store near my old apartment so that we could eat it with Philaylack and Nam. When Philaylack came to our room with Nam, we put on a pretense of normality. The room was very tidy, Fon and I spoke kindly to each other and we even pushed ourselves to eat some chicken. Nam looked so cute eating the chicken. The crispy parts were too hard for her, so Philaylack gave her small pieces of chicken meat to eat. She held a small piece of chicken in her hand and sucked on it like a lollipop. The thought of Fon's brother coming to our room had made me very nervous, but we actually passed a really enjoyable hour together. After Philaylack and Nam left, Fon had a quick shower and went to bed. I hadn't planned on sleeping just yet, but it had been several hours since I had last smoked candy and I had a belly full of chicken inside me, so I felt optimistic about my chances of getting some sleep.

I woke up the next day to a knock on the door. It was Ting. Fon let him in. Fon was fully dressed and her hair was wet, so I guessed that she had just come out of the shower. On the floor there was a gun and an empty carton of instant noodles.

"Ting leave now," Fon said to me. "You want to buy before he go?"

I still felt half asleep. I didn't even have time to think about whether I wanted to smoke straight away or not, but I didn't want to miss this chance. I bought five candies.

"Eat noodles before you start smoking," Fon said, pointing to a cup of instant noodles alongside my travel kettle.

I sat alongside Fon and I started making a boat out of the foil that Fon had removed from a packet of chewing gum.

"I'm not hungry," I said. "I had chicken before I went to bed. I'll eat later."

"Noy come now," Fon said.

"Which Noy?"

"Ladyboy Noy."

"Which ladyboy Noy? There are so many."

"Maybe you know her from Samlo or Don Chan."

"Is it the Noy ladyboy with the big fringe down to her eyes?"

"No."

"Is it Noy Num?"

'Num' has a few meanings in Lao, but one of them is 'breasts'. There was one ladyboy I knew from Samlo who had fake breasts. She was one of the very few ladyboys in falang town who had breast implants, so her nickname was 'Noy Num'.

"No. You will see when she come."

"Why is she coming here?"

"She give me candy before. Ting told me she no have money now so I want to share candy with her. Is it okay she come here?"

"Sure, whatever, but after that we will go to the clinic, right?"

"Yes, you have money?"

"I'll get it on the way there," I said.

Fon picked up the gun and placed it on her thigh. She seemed to be thinking carefully about what to say next.

"Where you go?" she asked me.

"To the clinic with you."

"I go alone."

I wanted to go to the clinic with Fon and pay the clinic directly, but the day before when Fon mentioned the unbelievable price of three

225

hundred dollars, I knew that she wouldn't let me pay the clinic directly. I figured she would try to get the three hundred dollars from me first, pay the clinic when I wasn't there, and then pocket the rest of the money.

"You shouldn't go alone. I want to go with you," I insisted.

Fon scrunched up her used boat and went to the bathroom to throw it down the toilet.

"I need to go home first," Fon said, when she sat back down on the floor.

"Why?"

"Maybe I need to show ID. I go home first and get it."

"Okay. Let's go to your home together and then we can go to the clinic."

"No. If you go home with me, mom and dad try to make us stay again. I will get ID and leave quickly. Better you no go."

I didn't really understand her point, but it wasn't worth arguing about.

"Okay. Then you go home to get your ID and then come back here and we can go to the clinic together. I can go out to get the money while you are getting your ID."

"I need money first."

"Why?"

It should have been very easy for Fon to give a reason if there was one, but she hesitated for a few moments.

"I need money first," she repeated.

"Why? I don't understand."

226

No answer.

Fon wouldn't go home to get her ID unless I gave her the money first, and I didn't want to hand over any money until we were in the clinic. We were at a stalemate. In the end I gave in, even though I knew that she was tricking me. I could have stood my ground and we both would have ended up staying in the room for the next few days arguing about it, but I just thought it was worth paying three million kip to get all this over with.

"Fon, I'll give you the three million kip first," I told her, "but don't call me later asking for more money. For example, after you get your ID, if you go the abortion clinic without me and then you suddenly tell me that it is four million kip, then I will not pay. No matter what happens, I will not give you any more money. Do you understand?"

"Yes. When you give?"

"And if you spend any of the three million kip on anything else, I will not give you more money. Even if you get 200,000 kip worth of fuel for your car and you need money to make up the three million kip, I will not give it to you, so don't ask. I mean it. Do you understand?"

"Yes. When you give?"

"I'll go to the ATM now."

"Then I need 200,000 kip for fuel for my car too."

When I came back from the ATM machine, there was a ladyboy sitting on the floor in the middle of the room with her back turned to me. Fon was doing her makeup in the mirror. The ladyboy turned to me.

"Hi Walt," she said, in a high voice.

I recognized Noy straight away. It was Noy Num – the Noy with

227

breast implants. She was a regular at Samlo and we often played pool together. When I had to describe her to another falang once, I referred to her as 'Barcelona Noy' because I often saw her in Samlo wearing nothing more than a Barcelona jersey that her ex-boyfriend had given her. The jersey was quite big, so it reached down passed her ass.

I handed the money to Fon. As soon as she got the money she started packing up her things.

"Are you going now?" I asked, surprised that Fon was leaving so quickly.

"Yes."

"What about Noy?" I whispered to Fon.

"She smoke here and then she go."

"How long will you be?"

"I don't know."

"Call me when you leave your house, and don't go to the clinic without me."

Fon looked around the room.

"Clean and throw away everything when you finish smoking," she said, and then, after a few words with Noy, Fon left.

It felt weird to be in the room alone with Noy. I didn't understand why Fon had asked her to come, and why didn't she leave with Fon? Perhaps Fon asked her to stay and keep an eye on me.

Noy and I both smoked quickly. We didn't speak much as we smoked. Within thirty minutes all the candy was gone. We sat back and turned on the air conditioner. Noy took the gun and put it under the sink in the bathroom. She wrapped the used boats up in a piece of tissue and flushed them down the toilet. I wanted more candy, so I called Ting. He said that it would be another forty minutes before he could come. I asked him to bring a couple of bottles of Beer Lao and some ice.

"Ting will be here in forty minutes," I said.

"Yes, yes," Noy said. "Now is relax time."

Noy opened up a new packet of cigarettes. She took the twenty cigarettes in her fist and placed them carefully on the tiled floor to her left. Neither of us smoked. I had bought the cigarettes because the foil inside the box was useful for making boats.

"Scissors?" Noy asked

"On the coffee table."

Noy placed the cigarettes carefully back in the box and dropped them into an empty plastic bag alongside the coffee table. She sat across from me on the floor and she began to make boats to pass away the time. She wasn't as meticulous as Fon. Noy barely took a minute to make a boat. Whereas Fon seemed to make boats to avoid talking with me, Noy made boats to keep busy. She looked at peace doing her job. Noy was tall and slim, and she was in full makeup. She had a very high nose and a sharp jaw, which made me think that her breasts were not the only work she had got done.

"My boyfriend come next week," Noy announced, to break the silence. "I stay with him two weeks. We go all round Laos."

"Good," I said, genuinely pleased for her. "It will be good to get away from candy for a while."

229

"Yes, relax time."

We had plenty of time left to kill before Ting came and I wanted to keep talking with Noy. I didn't want to lay in bed worrying about all the different ways Fon might screw me over.

"When did you become a ladyboy, Noy?"

"A long time ago. Me and friend take tablets when we fourteen."

"What tablets? Hormones?"

"No, not hormones. Different. You know when lady no want to have baby, but want to have sex. Tablet."

"Oh. You mean contraceptive pill. Why did you start taking them?"

"To be ladyboy. That pill make soft skin, pretty face, no muscle if you take it long time. If take it very young, it very good and make very pretty. I wish I take it when I twelve, but I a little old when I start, so I not very pretty. But my cock big and strong.....sometime."

"But why did you want to be a ladyboy?"

"Because even I very young I feel like girl, so I want to be pretty."

"So you are still taking the pills now?"

"Yes, sometimes, but now I not take 'cause my boyfriend come next week. I want my cock big and strong for him. He like," she said, and then she let out an abrupt burst of laughter. "I take tablet and cock no strong."

"When did you first come to Vientiane?"

"I was 16. I come work for my aunt. She have DVD shop in Talat Sao. I work in her shop and I stay her home. I don't know falang. I don't know candy. I don't know falang bar or anything."

"But now you know."

"Yes, now I know very well."

"What happened?"

"When I work in aunt shop, I no speak English. Just some words. But many falang go to Talat Sao, so I try speak some English with them. Sometime falang buy many DVDs for big price so my aunt very happy, so I want learn more English. Sometimes falang man look at me in bad way. Girl falang always very friendly and smile me, but some man look me in very sexy way. I can see. But I am very shy then. But one very nice man come shop many time, so we are friend. He want dinner with me at night, so I go with him. Next day, he want me go with him to see many things in Vientiane. So he give my aunt ten dollar and me ten dollar. Not big money, but we go nice places and eat nice food and drink some beer together in falang bar. He very good man. I like him very much. A little old, but a little handsome. He go many places in Laos and study butterflies in countryside. But he stay in Vientiane for one month."

"Is he the same boyfriend that is coming to visit you next week?"

"No, no. Different. This long time ago. He go home to France, and he no come back Laos. But one, two time he send money, Western Union, to help me a little. I no lie to him, but he want to help me. But that long time ago. I no contact him long time."

"So after he went back to France, you started going to falang bars alone? Samlo?"

"Yes, I go Samlo and Bor Pen Nyang. When I go to falang bar

231

with him, we meet many people. We play pool and we have fun many people. So I make friends. I speak with falang man, Lao lady, Lao ladyboy, so next time I go alone but I not shy because I know many people already. Sometime I meet nice man and they bring me hotel and they give me money. I no ask for money, but they give. I work with aunt in the day and I go falang bar at night. It fun, but my aunt angry a little, so I move to cheap room with two ladyboys – Cindy and Noy - Noy with hair to her eyes. You know, right?"

"Yes, I know that Noy and also Cindy from Samlo."

"Yes. They are my friends long time. Before, I go to Samlo or Bor Pen Nyang every night because I have money, but in falang bar Beer Lao twenty thousand kip – two dollar. Expensive. I buy one beer every night, maybe it sixty dollar one month – expensive more than room money. So I only go bar sometime. I walk on street and meet man sometime. I wait on corner across Khop Chai Deu. Many ladyboys wait there at night. You know. We see you every night before. You eat in restaurant and you walk to Samlo. Same every night. We see you."

"I used to eat dinner in Noi's Restaurant every night and then I used to go to Samlo, but that all stopped when I started smoking. No more eating."

"Yes. Yes," Noy agreed calmly. "You fat then, and cute, but now very skinny."

"So how did you get money for breasts?"

"I go work in Pattaya sometimes. Ladyboy work in Pattaya get big money – more than Laos. I not pretty, I no have breasts and I no skinny when I go Pattaya, but I get man every night. No problem. I give money family and I save money to make breasts. One England man and a South Africa man also give me money for breast operation. After I have breast I feel very good. Very sexy and look good too. I buy many sexy new clothes and very easy to get man if I have breast. But I no like Pattaya. I want to stay Laos, so I come home. One year, I go Pattaya maybe two months, make big money and come home."

"Why don't you like Pattaya? You said you can make a lot of money there?"

"I can make money, but Pattaya very dirty and crazy and expensive. I no like."

"Candy is expensive in Pattaya, right?"

"Yes, but I no smoke candy in Pattaya. I go Pattaya first time, I no smoke anything. No drug. Many ladyboy smoke, but I no want. I want money for breast operation. But two year ago I smoke ice with friend on her birthday. Me first time. I smoke ice and everything feel good. Sex so good when I smoke ice, feel so good," Noy said, and the thought of good sex made her so happy that she closed her eyes and smiled widely. "So I start smoke ice sometime. Ice very expensive. I go falang, and some falang want party with ice, so I help them buy and we smoke together. And sometimes I buy with friend too. In Pattaya, ladyboy make big money, but use big money too. I no like. "

"But ice is expensive in Laos too, right?"

"Yes, very expensive, but candy very cheap. Two dollar – same Beer Lao in falang bar."

"You have enough money to buy candy every day?" I asked, hoping that she wouldn't be offended by my question.

"Sometime I no have, but I friend Ting long time. I no have money, he give me a little candy. No problem. And sometime I can jam ('jam' is the Lao word for 'pawn') phone or falang camera or falang watch. If I no smoke candy, I very tired and I sleep for two days, so no make money. If smoke candy I have big energy and very horny so I can make money. And if smoke candy, I no eat, so very skinny and sexy."

"I didn't know you steal from falang. I know Cindy does. One time she asked me to buy a phone she robbed from a falang."

"I no want to steal from falang, but sometime I have no choice. Sometime easy steal, so I steal. But I not do many time. It make many problems. But I no steal from you. Don't worry. You friend."

Suddenly I remembered witnessing a confrontation between Noy and a young falang in one of my old guesthouses. I passed Noy and the falang on the stairway. Noy was sitting down on the stairs with her arms folded on her knees, staring blankly ahead. The falang was pleading with her to give back his camera because he had pictures of his family and his trip on it. Noy looked exhausted. It looked like she had been listening to him for hours.

"I sell it already," I heard Noy saying, as I walked down the stairs.

When Ting came, I bought ten candies. I kept five for myself and I gave five to Noy.

"Where Fon?" Ting asked me.

"Fon went home. She come back soon," I said.

"You sure?" he asked, with a grin on his face.

I shrugged my shoulders. Ting and Noy started speaking in Lao so I lay on the bed and gave Fon a call. She didn't answer. I sent her a message asking where she was. I took out my wallet and counted my cash. This was the last of my money. My bank account was now completely empty. I knew that the money would only last me a few days and then I would have to call my mom and ask her to deposit money into my account.

Fon didn't reply to my message. I called her again. No answer. Ting said he was going out to buy beer for us but he never came back. I guess he got a call from a customer suddenly. Keith came to my room to smoke with me and Noy for a while. We hadn't seen each other since Fon's family turned up at our guesthouse. I told Keith about the pregnancy tests, the clinic and the three million kip.

"She's taking you for a ride, mate," he concluded. "You need to get away from her."

I couldn't disagree with him. Keith, Noy and I sat on the floor in a circle. We each held our own boat, but we passed the gun around.

"Are you still with Sarah?" I asked.

"No, we broke up a few days after you went to stay with Fon's family. I met a new girl a few nights ago in Samlo. She smokes too. It's much easier. Maybe you know her. Her name is Ka."

"Yeah, I know Ka. Frizzy hair? Usually wears a white vest and tight jeans?

"That's her."

"Where is she now?"

"She's in my room with her mate. Her mate's name is Noy and she is really really short. She says she knows you."

"There are so many people called Noy around. I'm not sure which one you're talking about."

"Anyway, she is interested in you, so if you are around tonight, come to Bor Pen Nyang with us."

"I'll have to see what happens with Fon, but I doubt I'll be able to go."

As soon as Keith left, I gave Fon a call. She answered.

"Where are you?" I asked. "You left here about four hours ago."

"I stay in guesthouse near your old apartment."

I felt so frustrated because I couldn't control anything about this situation.

"Why are you in a guesthouse?" I asked. "You said you will go to the clinic."

"I cannot go today. I not feel good. I stay in guesthouse tonight and I go clinic soon."

"So why didn't you just come back here? Why did you go to a guesthouse?"

"Cause you no want me there."

I pulled the phone away from my ear and took a long deep breath to calm myself down.

"Which guesthouse are you in?"

Fon didn't know the name of the guesthouse, but from her description I knew it was the dodgy guesthouse near my old apartment that Keith and I had gone to one night looking for candy. I told Noy that I had to leave.

"Where you go?" she asked. "I have friend's scooter. I bring you."

I described the guesthouse to Noy, and of course she knew the one I was talking about. Everybody who did candy in and around falang town knew that dodgy guesthouse.

Before we got on the scooter, Noy made a phone call. When she finished the call, she said to me, "My friends with Fon in guesthouse. I go Fon room too and we smoke together."

"What friends?" I asked.

"Noy and Cindy."

Noy only had one helmet. She kindly offered it to me, but I insisted that she wear it.

"Why is Fon in a guesthouse with Cindy and Noy?" I asked, as we pulled away from my guesthouse.

"Because they smoke together."

"I know, but why are they together now? I thought Fon went home."

"Don't know."

What I really wanted to know was why Fon was in that dodgy guesthouse smoking candy with two ladyboys who she barely knew.

12

Fon was staying in the corner room on the second floor of the guesthouse. Cindy let us into the room. Thai pop music was playing on the TV to drown out the sound of the bubbling water in the gun. The corner room was bigger than the other rooms in this guesthouse. As well as a double bed, there was a makeup desk alongside the bathroom door, and there were two armchairs alongside the bed. Noy with the hair down to her eyes was sitting on one of the armchairs and Fon was sitting at the edge of the bed, fiddling with the one thousand kip note in the gun. I sat down alongside her. I could tell that she had been home because she was wearing different clothes to earlier that day, and even her bag in the corner was different.

"You're still smoking," I said.

Fon didn't react.

"What are you doing here?" I asked.

"I say already on phone," Fon mumbled.

Now that she had the one thousand kip note in the perfect position, at the perfect angle, she was ready to smoke. She lifted up her right leg towards her chest and placed the gun on her knee. She held it there with her mouth. Then she picked up the gun with her left hand and a lighter with her right hand. She placed the boat right under the end of the one thousand kip note and placed the lighter under the boat. A small pink pill sat in the middle of the beautifully made foil boat, but once she turned on the lighter the pretty pink pill started to melt into a thick, black tar-like substance and smoke started rising up. Even though the room was incredibly hot, the fan was turned off. Still air is very important in this situation because if there is any breeze, it will interrupt the flow of the smoke from the boat to the end of the one thousand kip note.

"Why didn't you go to the clinic?" I asked, after Fon had exhaled the smoke.

"I no want to go today, but I go soon. Don't worry."

"When?"

"Soon."

"Who bought the candy?"

"Me"

"With what money? And who paid for this room?"

"This my room, and I pay for the candy."

"With what money?"

"With my money. I still have three million kip for clinic. Don't worry. I know you only think about clinic and not about me."

"How can you pay for all this and still have three million kip?"

"When I in home today my brother give me money?"

"Today I withdrew all my money. I have nothing left in my bank, so I really can't give you any more money. I gave you three million kip. That should be more than enough for the clinic."

"I know. You say many times."

239

Fon stayed in that guesthouse for a whole week. Cindy, Noy with the fringe and Noy Num stayed in the room next to her. I spent most of that week with Fon. I only went back to my room a couple of times to change clothes. Fon and I had sex one time in her room. It was the first time since we had sex in the middle of the night in her parents' home. The surprising thing was that I could clearly see that Fon's breasts had become noticeably bigger. Up until then I had always wondered whether Fon was actually pregnant, but after seeing how her body had changed, I could put those doubts to one side.

Every day I begged Fon to stop smoking and go to the clinic. Fon had to pay for the room and she bought a lot of candy for herself and sometimes for the three ladyboys too. I kept asking her how she got money to pay for it all, but she just told me not to worry and that she still had the three million kip for the clinic. It was hard to believe.

"Can I see the three million kip?" I asked her one day.

"It's in my home. I'll go home and get it before I go clinic."

The three ladyboys usually came to Fon's room a couple of times a day to borrow makeup, to chat, to smoke with Fon, to share some food or to use Fon's phone to call Ting. One day I ran into Noy Num downstairs when I was on my way to buy water. She was with a Chinese-American middle-aged guy. She wanted to talk to me about something, so she gave him the key and he went up to her room first.

"Yesterday I hear Fon say something about you," Noy said.

"What did she say?" I asked, my heart suddenly pumping with

excitement at the possibility of finally exposing Fon's lies about the pregnancy.

"She talk about the baby."

"What did she say?" I asked.

Noy suddenly looked hesitant. She was holding her left hand to the side of her body, squeezing it tightly.

"I no want to say."

"Please, Noy, what did she say?"

"Fon and the baby is not what you think it is."

"What do you mean?"

"It is different to what she told you."

"So tell me. What did she say?"

Noy hesitated again. I asked her again about what she had heard Fon say, but now Noy seemed very reluctant to say anything more.

"Noy, I know you a long time from Samlo. We are friends. Please, please tell me. It's important to me. I need to know," I pleaded desperately.

Noy kept looking up at the sky, taking deep breaths.

"I cannot say," Noy said, looking genuinely sorry.

"Please, Noy," I pleaded one more time, but she had already decided not to tell me anymore. She turned away from me and went back to her room.

I made an effort not to argue with Fon while she stayed in the guesthouse, even though I had plenty of reasons to be angry with her. I was disgusted with her because I was sure I was not the father of the baby, and on top of that she was using the situation to get money from me. I knew that she was paying for the guesthouse and the candy with the three million kip that I had given her, but I simply didn't have any way to stop her. I was also sure that when she did eventually end up going to the clinic she would try to get more money from me.

One afternoon, Fon suddenly mumbled under her breath, "I go to clinic today."

I sat down alongside her.

"Really? You will definitely go today?" I asked.

"Yes. Can I stay with you when it finished?"

"Yes, of course."

"Okay. I check out of here and bring my things your room before I go."

"And then let's go to the clinic together," I said.

"I go home first. My money is in home and I need some clothes."

"I can go with you."

"No, I want go home alone. You wait in guesthouse and I call you when I leave home. But I don't have all three million kip."

I knew this moment would come.

"How much do you have left?" I asked.

"One hundred and fifty dollars. Can you give one hundred and fifty more? I give you again tomorrow, I promise. I'll ask my friend in France to send Western Union."

"Fon, I told you I would not give you more money for the clinic. Why did you spend the money?"

242

She didn't give a reason.

"There's no way I'm giving you more money," I insisted.

"Then I don't know what to do," Fon mumbled pathetically.

I could only think of one compromise.

"If we go to the clinic together and we pay one hundred and fifty dollars each, at the same time, then it's okay."

"Then you will pay?"

"Yes, but if you go to the clinic without me, get the abortion and then call me to come pay the one hundred and fifty dollars, then I won't do it. I mean it. I will never do that. I promise. It will never happen, so don't even think about that option."

I really emphasized this point because I truly believed that she had no money left, and that the one hundred and fifty dollars she wanted me to pay was the full price of the procedure. I had given her three hundred dollars for the procedure only a week earlier and she decided to spend it on candy and a room in a guesthouse, so there was no way I was going to give her any more money, no matter what.

I helped Fon pack up her stuff and then she dropped me back to my guesthouse on her way home. She promised to pick me up in about two hours, and then we would go to the clinic together. While I was waiting for Fon, I simply took a shower and rested on the bed. I tried to empty my mind completely and let my body rest. After two hours, I gave Fon a call. I knew she wouldn't answer. She didn't reply to my messages either. I kept calling her. Eventually she called me.

"Where are you?" I asked her, annoyed.

"I'm in the clinic."

I covered the phone microphone with my hand, turned away and screamed, "Bitch!!!"

I had to take a few deep breaths before I put the phone to my ear again.

"You're in the clinic?" I asked calmly.

"Yes, everything is finished. I need you come pay one hundred and fifty dollars. Ting pick you up now and bring you here."

"I'll go there, but I won't pay."

"You said you can pay one hundred and fifty dollars," Fon said, suddenly sounding very frustrated.

"I said I will pay it if we go to the clinic and pay the money together."

"I pay one hundred and fifty dollars already. But they need one hundred and fifty more," Fon sounded desperate.

I didn't know what to say. I just left the silence hang there for a few seconds.

"Ting go your guesthouse now. Go down stairs and wait him," Fon instructed me.

As I rode on the back of Ting's scooter, I thought about what I should do. I thought about what Keith had said to me the week before; 'She's taking you for a ride, mate.' He was right. I felt pathetic for giving her all that money for the clinic when I knew full well that I wasn't the father, and then she took the piss out of me by smoking the money away right in front of me. I told myself that no matter what might happen, no matter what I might see in the clinic, I would not hand over any money to Fon or the clinic. I was absolutely resolute on this point.

Ting pulled over at the side of the road about five minutes from my guesthouse, in front of a row of small stores. Some of the stores were closed because it was after six o'clock, but there was a small grocery store and a perfume store still open.

"Why did you stop?" I asked Ting.

"That the clinic," Ting said, pointing to the premises alongside the clothes store.

It didn't look like a clinic. It looked too small and rundown to be a place where medicine is practiced. The sign above the door was written in the Lao alphabet, but among it all I saw the word 'Clinic'.

"Are you coming in?" I asked Ting.

"No, I go see customer now."

I watched Ting drive off. It was only then that I noticed Fon's green car parked outside. The reception area was very small, providing only enough space for a reception desk and two wooden chairs placed against the wall. The floor was bare concrete so it didn't feel like a normal clinic. There weren't any windows or air conditioners. The entrance was left open and there was a roof fan to keep the space cool. There wasn't anybody at reception, but there was a bell. A few seconds after I rang it, a nurse appeared from around the corner.

"Fon," I said, but she already knew who I had come to see. The nurse brought me to the room directly behind the reception. It was a bleak room, without any decorations or touches of care. There were simply two

245

hospital beds in the room and nothing else. Fon was lying on the bed nearest the door. I was shocked when I saw her. She was lying on the bed in a blue hospital robe, in a pool of blood. Lao hospital beds consist of a metal frame and a dark blue mattress. These mattresses are not covered in lovely bed clothes like in hospitals in the west. They are non-absorbent and can easily be cleaned by a quick wipe down with a wet towel. The mattress didn't absorb anything, so Fon's blood formed a pool around her lower back. Her gown was covered in blood. When she moved, the puddle of blood moved too and drops of blood dripped from her gown. *How can they just leave her like this?* I thought to myself.

I placed my hand on Fon's arm and asked her sincerely how she was feeling.

"Weak," she said.

We talked briefly about how the procedure went and about Fon's body condition.

"Please pay and let's go," Fon said, in a tired voice.

I sat down on the chair alongside her bed.

"I told you, I'm not paying," I said.

Fon let out a tired sigh.

"What you mean you not pay?" she asked. "You say you pay."

"You know what I said. I told you I wouldn't pay if you come without me and then ask me to come and pay the money separately."

"I pay half already. If I no pay half, they no help me. I could not wait for you to come. I wanted to do quickly. What the problem?"

I wanted to tell her that I didn't believe her, that I was sure that the whole procedure was only one hundred and fifty dollars, not three hundred dollars like she claimed. But it wasn't the right time or place for that kind of talk. I just told Fon simply that I wouldn't pay. I considered going out to the reception and asking how much the procedure cost, but I decided against it because I thought the nurse would not speak English, it might make Fon angry, and, also, I thought it was entirely possible that Fon had asked them to lie for her if I was to ask any questions.

Fon and I stayed in silence for what seemed like quarter of an hour. She was waiting for me to give in.

"What can I do?" she asked. "I promise them I pay half before and then my boyfriend come and pay half. So they say okay. You say you will pay."

"I didn't. You know I didn't."

"I give you back tomorrow. I call France man and he send money. If you no pay, it will be big problem. Please. What? I have to call my family and my family come again and see me like this. You okay. You go back home soon and forget everything, but my family never forget this if they see me. My life over already. Just pay and let me go home, please."

"I gave you money for the clinic already," I replied.

"That day I no ready to come, and I needed money to live."

"But why didn't you just come here with me today, like we agreed? I told you I wouldn't pay more if you did it like this."

"You say you will pay."

There was another long silence.

I was completely torn. Despite my cold words to Fon, of course I wanted to help her. I had never seen anybody as vulnerable and pathetic as Fon was in that moment, as she lay on the bed in a pool of blood. She looked pale and helpless. I wanted to just pay the one hundred and fifty dollars and get out of there. I had the money in my wallet. I could have easily paid, but it wasn't about the money. It was about pride. It was about winning and losing. There were moments during the long silences when I was on the verge of giving in and reaching into my pocket to pull out my wallet, but in those moments I reminded myself that Fon had manufactured this situation because she assumed that I would feel sorry for her, and that I would pay in the end. This assumption gave her the freedom to spend the three hundred dollars I had given her for the clinic. She assumed she could get more out of me if she forced me into this corner.

The silence continued until a nurse came in and said something in Lao. Fon was sitting upright on the bed, looking blankly at the door.

"What did she say?" I asked Fon, after the nurse left.

"They are closing," Fon mumbled.

A few minutes later, Fon got out of the bed and walked out to the reception. Drops of blood fell from her gown onto the concrete floor. She spoke with the nurse and the receptionist for a few minutes. I couldn't understand a word of what they were saying. They let Fon leave. Outside the clinic Fon took her bag of clothes out of her car and went back into the clinic. I didn't follow her back inside. I figured she had some money in her bag and that she was going back in to pay, but I guess I was wrong, because when she came back she didn't have her car keys with her. She walked past her car.

"What's happening?" I asked Fon, as I followed a few steps behind her.

I had to ask Fon this question a few times before she said anything.

"Can I go your room?" she asked.

"Yes, of course. Why didn't you bring your car?"

"I no have money to pay clinic so I give them my car key. I come back when I have money."

"But you can't walk all the way back to the guesthouse. Let's try to get a tuk-tuk."

Fon started sobbing quietly as she walked along the street in her bloody hospital gown. Fortunately, the street was empty. It took me a few minutes to look passed the bloody gown and notice that she was walking barefoot. Fon refused to stop and wait for a tuk-tuk, and she pulled her arm away sharply when I tried to carry her bag for her. It took us about thirty minutes to walk all the way back to the guesthouse. As soon as we entered the room, Fon changed her clothes and went to bed. She stayed in bed for two full days, only waking up a couple of times to use the bathroom and drink water. After that, things got back to normal. She started smoking again and she got money from her 'friend' in France to get her car back.

During my last few weeks in Laos things got even worse between me and Fon. We had arguments that lasted several days at a time, and on a couple of occasions the staff in the guesthouse had to come to our room to tell us to keep our voices down. One day, a few days before I was due to leave Laos, I smoked two of Fon's candies while she was in the shower. She went crazy because I refused to replace the candies I had taken from her. She grabbed my bag with my laptop and several other things inside and stormed out of the room. I pleaded with Fon for several days to bring back my stuff, but she refused. On my last day in Laos I found the full name and phone number of Fon's French friend written on a scrap of paper in my wallet. I messaged this information to Fon. She must have been terrified that I would contact him because within a couple of hours she returned my stuff and we smoked together for one last time in my room. She even dropped me to the Laos-Thai border to catch my bus.

"Please don't make any trouble for me," Fon said, when we arrived at the border. "The French man is all I have now. And please don't come back here again. This place no good for you."

"I won't contact the guy in France," I assured her. "Take care of yourself."

I leaned over to kiss Fon goodbye. She turned her face away. I took my backpack out from the back seat and walked away. This time I didn't cry on the overnight bus to Bangkok. I was ready to leave Laos.

I am still in contact with Keith. He is back in England, working and getting on with his life. He still thinks about Laos a lot, but he knows he shouldn't go back there.

Fon moved to France and married the French guy.

Milton Keynes UK
Ingram Content Group UK Ltd.
UKHW041634240924
448733UK00002B/165